SIMPLY SPACED

Brimming with creative inspiration, how-to projects, and useful information to enrich your everyday life, Quarto Knows is a favorite destination for those pursuing their interests and passions. Visit our site and dig deeper with our books into your area of interest: Quarto Creates, Quarto Cooks, Quarto Homes, Quarto Lives, Quarto Drives, Quarto Explores, Quarto Gifts, or Quarto Kids.

First published in 2019 by Rock Point,
an imprint of The Quarto Group,
142 West 36th Street, 4th Floor
New York, NY 10018, USA
T (212) 779-4972 F (212) 779-6058
www.QuartoKnows.com

Rock Point titles are also available at discount for retail, wholesale, promotional, and bulk purchase. For details, contact the Special Sales Manager by email at specialsales@quarto.com or by mail at The Quarto Group, Attn: Special Sales Manager, 100 Cummings Center Suite 265D, Beverly, MA 01915 USA.

10 9 8 7 6 5 4 3

ISBN: 978-1-63106-607-8

Library of Congress Cataloging-in-Publication Data

Names: Leed, Monica, author.
Title: Simply spaced : clear the clutter and style your life / Monica Leed.
Description: New York, NY : Rock Point 2019. | Summary: "Simply Spaced will teach you methods and habits that will help shift your life from "overwhelmed" to "overjoyed" by sharing the principles of minimalism, streamlining, and simplifying--in style"-- Provided by publisher.
Identifiers: LCCN 2019019304
Subjects: LCSH: House cleaning. | Storage in the home. | Orderliness.
Classification: LCC TX324 .L44 2019 | DDC 648/.5--dc23
LC record available at https://lccn.loc.gov/2019019304

EDITORIAL DIRECTOR: Rage Kindelsperger
CREATIVE DIRECTOR: Laura Drew
MANAGING EDITOR: Cara Donaldson
SENIOR EDITOR: John Foster
INTERIOR DESIGN: Evelin Kasikov

Printed in China

SIMPLY SPACED

Clear the Clutter
and Style Your Life

MONICA LEED

ROCK
POINT

CONTENTS

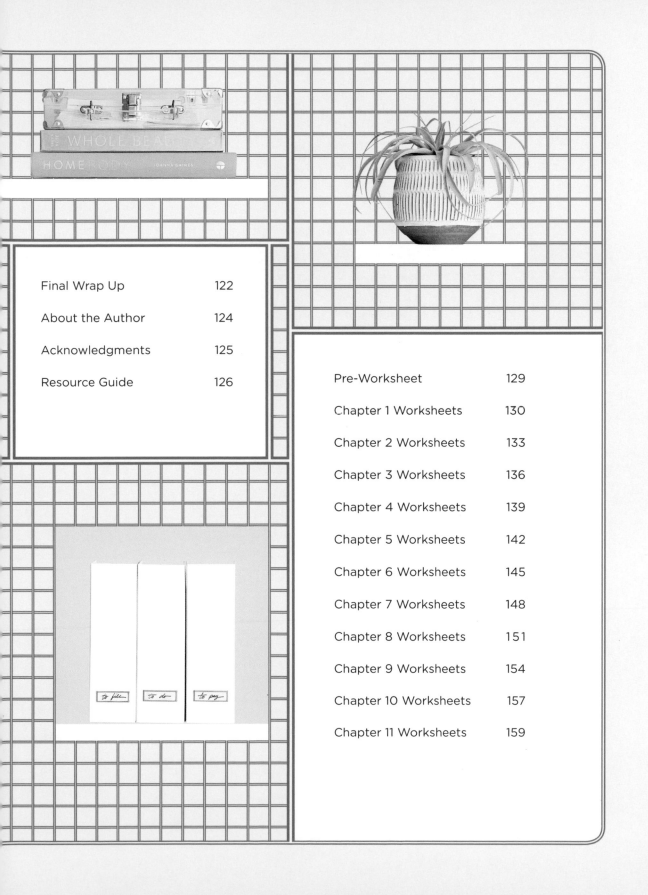

INTRODUCTION

Monica Leed

A LITTLE ABOUT ME

My name is Monica Leed, and I'm an art director, professional organizer, entrepreneur, and principal founder of Simply Spaced, LLC a professional organizing company headquartered in Los Angeles. With a background in design and ten years of work in the film industry, I've transferred my passion for efficient space design, time management, and the power of organizational systems into a growing company that helps people get organized across many areas of their lives. In 2011, life threw me an unexpected curve ball when I got in a serious car accident. At the time, I was living a hectic all-work-and-no-play lifestyle with an out-of-balance home life that left me feeling stuck and overwhelmed. The universe dealt me a blow and forced me to take a step back and focus on the things that mattered most, like my family, my husband, and my well-being. So, I decided to get rid of the inessential extraneous things in my life and I began, what organizers deem "decluttering," my home and life. In a time of healing, I started to clear out the physical clutter and, like magic, unearthed an entirely new perspective. I learned that *simplicity* wasn't just a trend, it was the catalyst for creativity. I wrote a screenplay. I launched a business and I learned that a less-is-more approach to life spoke to far more than the number of shoes in my closet.

My passion for creating livable spaces led me to professional organizing at a time when the field was really beginning to hit its stride. What I found missing from the newly-popularized decluttering movement, however, was any mention of *style*. After years of creating environments that told a story for fictional characters, I was drawn to the idea of helping real people curate their own spaces to reflect their real lives. I believe everyone deserves to live in a home that inspires creativity, calm, and purpose, regardless of its size.

You won't walk into my house on any given day and see it looking like my Simply Spaced Instagram feed (follow me if you don't already!), which is aspirational and showcases my organizational systems at their peak. The photos capture perfectly decluttered, tidied spaces that have been styled by a team of people over the course of several days in preparation of the photo shoot. Of course, this doesn't mean it's fake. It's real, just not *real life*.

Now that you know a bit about me, tell me about *you*. What is your story? What would your home tell me if I stepped through the front door? Also, do me a favor and stop apologizing for the imperfections and forget about ever being perfectly organized. Being organized is a journey, not a destination. You will never have all your stuff together—and what fun would that be anyway? The goal is to feel in control. People are so fascinated by the phenomena behind organization and tidying up right now, but as someone who has been doing this for seven years, I am not surprised at all. I know what it feels like to live in chaos, and I've also seen lives change when they take back control.

WHY GET ORGANIZED?

This is a common question we ask ourselves all the time. The truth is, most of us don't need perfectly folded clothes tucked neatly in color-coded drawers, but rather a relief from our frenetic, out-of-control, distracted lives. But how do we create such a serene lifestyle? Where does it start? The first step is to look at our home, since it is, by nature, a reflection of ourselves. How we set up our living space either supports, or thwarts, our flow. When we stop and really think about the sheer amount of time we spend in our homes, we soon see the significance of how it makes us feel. When out of balance, our home can drain energy and stymie our progress. However, when it is in alignment, our home becomes the energy source that propels us to realize our wildest dreams and live our most rewarding life. We are hard wired to crave three things: ease, order, and inspiration, and this book will give you everything you need to arrange your home to attract all three.

Yes, this is a blueprint for clearing clutter, but even more importantly, it's a guide to becoming aware of your relationship with your environment and how it affects your life. It's not enough to just declutter and give everything away without first committing to a shift in perspective and desire for clarity. You will see in the following pages that once you've cleared some space, you'll feel excited to create a home that feels beautiful and intentional, but my greatest wish is that you'll feel empowered. Your environment shapes, and sometimes dictates, how you feel and behave. My goals are to (1) draw attention to your habits and offer simple solutions that reduce feeling overwhelmed, and (2) help you to clear the physical *and* mental clutter that's holding you back, while giving you permission to be a hot mess in the process.

This book is meant to be a guide for those of us who often get caught up in a "bigger, better, someday" way of thinking. That is, a bigger house will solve all our problems, a better life exists elsewhere, or someday I will have a happy home. After six years of working as a professional organizer, I've learned that more space only means more headaches if you cannot get to the root of your mess. If you fail to get a handle on your clutter and get intentional about your shopping, you'll spend the rest of your life treading water in a bigger fish bowl. I challenge you to see the house you live in right now as an asset in your life, rather than the enemy, so let's take a moment for gratitude and commit to aligning with that ideal home now.

LET'S BE REAL

As with any organization project, you will certainly hit roadblocks. You may get frustrated; you may cry; and it probably won't be easy at first, but in this awareness, you'll unleash your intrinsic power. Once you get started, you will find yourself begin to let go of your attachments—and frustrations—and in the process learn some tips, experience unexpected joy, let go of negative energy, and move on to the important things life has to offer.

I know this process works because I have seen real-life results over the years with my clients. They got their houses in order and their lives changed. They conquered fears, birthed children, married, divorced, wrote books, launched careers, and realigned with their purpose. I'm so excited for it to happen for you. My hope is that you use these tools and concepts to shift your mindset

around clutter and accumulation. I'm teaching you a shorthand and giving you a handbook so that you can set up your house to run it like a boss.

Here's a scenario I have seen play out time and time again: one partner, usually the main breadwinner, decides to buy a house. All the money goes into that big and beautiful home. If there's money left over, it is used to buy furniture, a smaller amount is spent on styling and almost nothing is allotted to organization and maintenance. The responsibility of maintaining the house falls onto one domestic partner, who eventually becomes distraught over trying to balance the house's never-ending upkeep with his or her own personal life and career responsibilities, and everyone is overwhelmed, resentful, and feeling malaise at home. By domestic partner, I don't necessarily mean a non-working partner, since very often one person assumes the responsibility of domestic management while also working a full- or part-time job. So, what can be done? My goal is to convince you that the organizational systems you set up in your home are as important, if not *more* important, than the house itself. Without functional systems in place that align with how you live your life, it really is just a house. But when you become intentional about how you live, when you can find things and appreciate them, when you feel excited and not overwhelmed, that's when you know you are home.

HOW TO USE THIS BOOK

This book is designed to address each area of your home, one room at a time. Each chapter is dedicated to one specific project that will motivate and inspire you to move on to the next. First, we will begin with eight space-specific projects (kitchen, bathroom, closet, etc.). Then we will move on to the "specialty categories," my clients typically need the most help with. These include paper, photos, and mementos. Each specialty category has its own chapter and unique process. I suggest that you collect these items as you work through your spaces so that you can attack each project holistically. Things in your life may begin to change as you start to declutter. You are physically shifting energy, and since you too are an energetic being, don't be surprised if you find your own power alongside that adaptor you have been searching for.

THE METHOD: SIMPLIFY, STREAMLINE, STYLE

This book is a blueprint to my three-pronged method that takes the guesswork out of getting organized: Step 1, **Simplify**; Step 2, **Streamline**; and Step 3, **Style**. Each chapter will apply these three prongs to the designated area. I'm sharing my method that I use as a professional organizer in my clients' homes. My hope is that you, too, will learn the process so that you can tackle any space or project with complete confidence. And in doing so, you will release your fear and attachment to perfection. Follow these steps and be prepared to do the work. I promise you clarity and calm await you on the other side. Let's learn a bit more about each step and what it will entail.

STEP 1: SIMPLIFY

The first step in any organizing project is to declutter and downsize. The process involves pulling everything out, grouping like-with-like, and discarding anything that you no longer love, need, or use. This may just be the most transformational step. By clearing out the clutter and only holding onto items that bring value to your life, you will immediately feel an energetic shift in your home. By clearing the physical clutter, you're one step closer to obtaining clarity of mind and purpose, so let the decluttering begin.

1. Complete worksheet 1

Connecting with your "why" will keep you motivated, because you can keep the bigger picture in mind as the process gets challenging. Each chapter has three corresponding worksheets and checklists (see pages 129–160) that correspond to each Simplify, Streamline, and Style process to help you become really clear about your intentions for each project and space in your home. The worksheets are perforated, so you can tear them out and have them at your side while you tackle each chapter. I encourage you to dedicate a notebook for your Simply Spaced journey, as you'll be taking lots of notes along the way. You can also use your notebook to complete the worksheet questions or hop over to our website (simplyspaced.com/worksheets) and print out downloadable worksheets too. You will learn more about the worksheets and will complete your first one at the end of this introduction (see page 18).

2. Set up your workspace

Gather your tools: A notebook, pen, Sharpie, Post-it notes, trash bags, and four to five large boxes, or bins, are all you need to get started. Other tools that may come in handy include:

- Measuring tape
- Brown paper bags
- Binder clips
- Rubber bands
- Label maker and tape

TO SIMPLIFY

▷ **START HERE**

1. Complete worksheet 1.
2. Set up your workspace.
3. Pull everything out and group like-with-like.
4. Process your items.
5. Wrap up.

Why are tools important?

Tools help you stay organized and create a framework for the entire process. Using something as simple as a Post-it to identify categories or a notebook to capture your thoughts frees your brain so you can find your flow. Remember, our brains are factories, not filing systems. It seems so elementary, and yet that simple transference of information is incredibly powerful.

> **PRO TIP:** Practice using Post-its in other areas of your life to prove to yourself how powerful they can be. Research shows that when we are asked to do something via a Post-it, we are more likely to act. This simple tool is a reprieve from our technologically-saturated, overly-demanding world. A Post-it can filter through the noise of it all.

Label your bins

Donate, Recycle, Trash, and Other Room. The "Other Room" bin is for any item you come across that belongs in another room, so that you're not wasting energy running back and forth between spaces. This will allow you to stay focused on just one room. As you start to sort, you'll come across items that you may need to repair, return, sell, or send to Grandma Betty. Create more sub-set groupings of the items going out as they pop up.

> ### MEDITATE ON THIS: DONATIONS
>
> Research and contact three local charities where you can donate your items. Food banks, churches, women's centers, rehabilitation centers, and youth centers are all a great start. Make a call and a connection, and I promise your life will change.

3. Pull everything out and group like-with-like

You need an area where you can sort, like a kitchen island or dining room table. Or you can use your floor space or the bed, depending on what room you're working in. Depending on the level of clutter in your space, you may need to pull everything out of the room and to another space. Begin with visible clutter: countertops, floors, tables, any surface covered by stuff. Take everything out of the space you're working in and group by category. For example, if you're working in the kitchen, pull out all the pots and pans, place them on the table, group by type and use Post-its to identify the grouping. Categorizing this way allows you to see your collection in its entirety.

> ### MEDITATE ON THIS: SELLING ITEMS
>
> One of the hardest things to do is let go of something you spent a lot of money on. Use your own discretion on how to navigate this. But my professional advice is to always go back to the bigger picture. If your goal is to declutter, don't let things like "sunk costs" undermine your goal. Rarely is your time and energy worth the resale process.

4. Process your items

To truly curate your home's essentials, I recommend touching every item in the room. As you do, ask yourself, **"Do I love, need, or use this?"** If you're not likely to use or appreciate the item in the near future, place it in the "Donate" or "Recycling" bin. If an item really can't have a second life, thank it, give it a high five, or whatever you need to do to show gratitude, and place it in the trash. Consider adding a "To Sell" or "Maybe" pile as you move through the space to avoid wasting time deliberating. You can always bring in a friend to help you decide at the end. When you come across a new category item, label it with a Post-it immediately (remember, there is power in the Post-it). This will help you keep track as you get deeper into the project and keep you from becoming overwhelmed.

The goals here are to (1) keep only that which serves your current needs, (2) embrace quality over quantity, and (3) let go of stagnant reminders of the past. An object either raises your energy, depletes your energy, or is neutral. You may not *love* your cheese grater, but it falls into the neutral category; therefore, it's useful—those seventeen extras, just no.

15 THINGS TO LET GO OF NOW

I give you permission to donate, recycle, or toss the following:

1. Gifts you wish you never received (fish plate)
2. Items you *should* use . . . but don't (dusty home exercise equipment)
3. Items you "spent good money on" but don't use
4. Anything broken or inoperable (be honest: will you ever fix it?)
5. Anything permanently soiled or stained
6. Heirlooms that even they didn't love
7. Keepsakes that even you don't love
8. Dud duplicates
9. Anything expired
10. Uncomfortable clothing and shoes
11. Documents you can find online
12. Business cards (put that contact in your phone!)
13. Old cords and electronics
14. Books and magazines you'll never read
15. Promotional tote bags, mugs, and swag

HOW DO I DECIDE?

The most important question you will be asking yourself is, **"Do I love, need, or use this?"** If you can't decide, here are some other questions to ask yourself:

- Have I used this in the last year?
- If I were shopping right now, would I buy this?
- Is the only reason I have this item because I feel guilty for wasting money?
- Is the only reason I have this item because it was a gift and I feel bad getting rid of it?
- Is this item worth the amount of time it takes to maintain, fix, or store it?
- How many times has this item been moved from place to place without being used?
- Do I have a similar item that serves the same purpose?
- Do I have a realistic plan to use this?
- Does it suit my aesthetic?
- Does it support my goals?
- And last, but not least . . . do I hate this?

> **PRO TIP:** Set aside any reusable bins, boxes, containers, shelf risers, or receptacles that can be repurposed throughout this process. You may ultimately opt for streamlined storage, but the extra storage may come in handy.

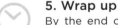

5. Wrap up

By the end of this "Simplify" step, you should have all the items in a room, or space, cleared out of drawers and shelves and off countertops. Yes, it gets worse before it gets better, and that's perfectly normal. The key is to empty everything out, decide what's leaving this space, and identify what's staying. Items should be grouped and labeled with a Post-it that indicates the category. Once this is complete, it's now time to remove "Trash" and "Recycle" bins and put away "Other Room" items. For your "Donation" pile, either drop them off or schedule a pick up. Finally, if you're taking a break before you dive into step 2, Streamline, and you need to live in and use this space in the meantime, temporarily move the items to another location.

> **PRO TIP:** Now that everything is out, this is a great time to do a deep clean, bring in a professional cleaning crew, or simply wipe down surfaces.

STEP 2: STREAMLINE

We have all heard the adage "A place for everything, and everything in its place." I want to illustrate this extremely important point: your home *can* be easy to navigate, if you've set up the proper systems. This "Streamline" step involves optimizing and maximizing space. Now that you've cleared the clutter, imagine what's possible in your space. I encourage you to think about under-utilized wall space and reimagine shelving, tools, and products that will add function to your room.

STREAMLINE

▷ **START HERE**

1. Complete worksheet 2
2. Create zones and categorize
3. Maximize space
4. Implement storage solutions
5. Label

1. Complete worksheet 2

Use worksheet 2 to guide you through the streamline process and identify what has, and has not been, working in the space.

2. Create zones and categorize

Duplicate your Post-it notes for each category you've identified (note: each chapter has a list of common categories that I use). Assign each category a new home by placing your duplicate Post-it notes in the optimal landing spot. This will require some trial-and-error. Ask yourself these questions:

- Is this the best location for this category to be stored?
- Will I remember that it's there?
- Will the items fit in this space?
- Does this landing spot make it easy to complete associated tasks?
- Can I easily get to frequently used items?
- Are similar categories stored next to each other?

3. Maximize space

Think about where items were inaccessible, crammed, or difficult to reach. These are the spaces that you'll focus your energy on. With a few minor adjustments and strategic placement of storage products, you'll clear up space and make items easier to retrieve. The idea of retro-fitting a closet or cabinet may sound daunting, but there are ample resources to help you expedite the project more efficiently.

PRO TIP: Hire an organizer to help you come up with storage solutions, a handyperson, carpenter, or one of the many retailers who offer free design services. Check out the Resource Guide (see page 126) for more ideas.

Adjust shelving as needed

Move adjustable shelves or add adjustable shelving to existing cabinets and notate where pull-out drawers can be installed for ease of access.

Inventory categories

Make an inventory of any items that need better storage. Keep a list in your notebook, which will help you when you look for product solutions.

Take measurements

Measure the width, depth, and height for the areas you plan to get bins, boxes, or shelves for to make sure your solution will fit.

Create a product list

Make a list of everything that comes to mind while you are taking inventory of what storage solutions will help you organize your things. Here are a few ideas:

- Add additional shelving
- Add furniture, like a bookshelf, dresser, or cabinet, if you're tight on storage space
- Replace a low shelving unit with a tall one
- Add floating shelves or hooks above an overstuffed area
- Use stackable bins or shelf risers to maximize space on a shelf or in a cabinet
- Attach hooks to the inside of a door
- Use baskets to store items in a deep cabinet or high shelf
- Insert dividers in drawers to keep contents separate
- Install turntables for hard-to-reach, high cabinets or deep drawers

Woven baskets are perfect stylish storage solutions.

Why do organizers love pull-out drawers, deep drawer bins, and baskets? Because we want to use every last inch of what you are working with while maintaining access. If it's out of sight, it's out of mind, and sometimes that's a good thing. If it's lost deep in a drawer somewhere, what is the point anyway? The right storage solution is the answer. For a list of my top picks for every space, visit www.simplyspaced.com/shop.

> **PRO TIP:** Call a handyperson or friend to help you assemble products, hang a shelf, or bring you a sandwich. Delegate like a boss and don't apologize for getting help; celebrate it (organizing takes energy)!

5. Label

One of the things Simply Spaced is known for is use of labels. Labels take the guesswork out of maintaining order in the systems you've created. Just like Post-its, they free up your brain so that you can focus on the important stuff. Well-planned, personalized labels add visual cohesion and a personal touch. Labels also empower other people who use your space to get on board with your systems. Spouses, kids, grandparents, roommates, housekeepers, houseguests, etc. can move around with more autonomy, comfort, and ease without asking where everything is. It also makes it easier for them to return things to their homes.

4. Implement storage solutions

A common misconception when it comes to organizing is that it's all about decluttering. While that is, of course, the number-one first step, implementing storage solutions is what makes your simplification sustainable. Sometimes you just need to buy some things, like bins, a lazy Susan, under-shelf storage, or some drawer dividers—these are an organizer's best friends. The right storage solutions can make or break your project, so choose wisely. When you implement your new solutions and put everything away, think about accessibility and ease of use.

> **MEDITATE ON THIS:**
>
> Keep in mind that your home is an ever-evolving ecosystem. Sometimes a little trial and error is required before everything feels just right. Be open to changing systems to better serve you and your loved ones.

STEP 3: STYLE

I believe that a home that looks and feels beautiful has a transformational effect on how people live in it. A space that is in order makes you feel in control. A space that's warm makes you feel a sense of ease. Transform your relationship with your home, and you will transform your relationship with yourself. Maintaining and caring for your home becomes second nature when it's a place you feel proud of. When your home is a visual reminder of your cherished memories, values, and aspirations, you will attract more of what you want into your life. That's why style matters. Now that you have done the hard work in steps 2 and 3 of Simplify and Streamline, it's time to have fun and get creative! There is no process here. Each chapter in this book will provide you with my best style tips for each project, but they are applicable anywhere. Before we move on to each area, here are some foundational style principles to think about before you dive in.

Define your style

Do you prefer modern, clean lines or natural woven fibers? Do you like a bohemian, more-is-more aesthetic or do you feel more at home in a space that's cozy with a Pacific Northwest vibe? Identifying your style can shape your choices throughout this process. If you're unsure of your preferences, it's time to *define* your style. Begin by collecting images of spaces, clothing, and designs that you love on Pinterest or a physical bulletin board. Then, edit it down. Pull out any images that don't feel in line with the rest. Once the collection is curated, take a step back and consider what elements all the pictures have in common. Next, you may want to start a board for each project that you take on (one for your kitchen, one for your bedroom, etc.). And head over to the Simply Spaced website at simplyspaced.com/stylequiz to take my style quiz.

Know your materials

Identify which materials you are tactilely drawn to. My favorites are wood, marble, terracotta, brass, metal, straw, wool, leather, glass, linen, canvas, wire, paper, and bamboo. I use this materials list as a reference when I shop so that I remember to bring in the materials that I love.

Feature what you love

To fuse your newly organized space with your personal style, showcase what you love. Gather special items that are currently on display or stowed away in another room. This could be a plant, painting, photograph, vintage T-shirt, or antique cooking utensil. Anything that uniquely represents you and brings a smile to your face is fair game. Consider what needs to be done to prepare the items for display. Sometimes this means framing a photo of your beloved grandmother or buying a wall mount for your guitar. Once these items are on display, make sure to appreciate them often.

Showcase and display your special items.

The rule of three

The rule of three is a helpful hack for styling your home. It's simple: things arranged in odd numbers are more appealing to the eye. A grouping of three is the magic number. Your space will feel less staged and more dynamic. People often think that for things to feel "orderly" they need to be lined up and even, but the opposite is true when it comes to style. Try mixing heights as a hack to create a quick vignette in any room.

Embrace white space

Most people have a natural tendency to fill every space and cover every surface, but this leaves no reprieve for the eye. Look at the pages in this book; stop reading for a moment, step back, and look at the two-page spread. Do you see how white space provides a framework for you to process and digest the text?

In your home, white space serves as a palette cleanser and allows you to appreciate the things you want to highlight or feature. I'm not talking about scarcity or sterility; I'm talking about leaving room for visual breath. Remember, this concept doesn't just apply to walls but also counters, mantles, shelves, dressers—just about every area of your living space.

Edit, edit, edit

Step back and look at your room. Does it feel balanced? Consider which items complement each other and if they tell your story. If anything is being overpowered or is in a wrong color palette, let it go or set it aside for another space. Remember, less is more, especially with decor. And keep in mind, your style is ever evolving. My guidance is intended to help you find *your* flow.

WORKSHEETS

As previously mentioned, at the end of this book, starting on page 129, you'll find worksheets and checklists for each step of my method designed to support your journey. To begin, complete the Pre-Worksheet. Then, complete the appropriate chapter worksheet before beginning each step to set your intention and to get in alignment. Connecting with your "why" will help you keep your eye on the bigger picture, even when the organization feels challenging.

As you move through the projects in this book, use your "why" to inform how you set up your home. Use it to guide the decisions you make as you encounter roadblocks. Clarifying this intention from the start will help you create a space that supports your dream life and gives you energy and motivation when you need it most.

SIMPLY SPACED STYLE HACKS

Here are some of my favorite style tips:

- Store nice-to-see items in transparent containers like jars, display cabinets, or clear bins
- Store bulk, backup, and unsightly items (we all have them) in concealed bins, boxes, or baskets
- Use cohesive bins, but mix up materials, textures, and colors to create a softer, more organic look
- Prioritize quality over quantity
- Place light, transparent items up high
- Store heavier items and materials down low
- Color-code items, such as clothing and books, to add visual interest
- Embrace white space to create visual calm

CELEBRATE SMALL WINS

When you're feeling overwhelmed, challenge yourself to organize one drawer, one bag, or one cabinet. Start small if going big feels unachievable. When you're done, take a picture, send it to your mom, share it on Instagram with #anorganizingstory, then go do your best "I'm a rockstar dance."

Summary

The tips and tools I provide are meant to guide you to new habits, perspectives, and insights from the vantage point of a professional organizer. There is no one-size-fits-all approach to organizing every space. I encourage you to practice grace, flexibility, and self-love as you move throughout these pages. Keep in mind that if you're following my method correctly, it will get worse before it gets better. I'm asking you to do the work now—this year—to save yourself time in the long run and over the course of your life. Getting organized doesn't happen overnight. But trust me, when you get to the place where everything in your house has a home and you can clean up in just a few minutes, you'll feel like you conquered the world!

Consider blocking off time, free of distractions, for each step in this process. You may need to break up each step into multiple work sessions. Dedicate a minimum of two to four hours to any size project you take on. Schedule it on your calendar, and then book a babysitter, turn off the television, and turn on your favorite playlist to get in the zone. With your full attention and a bit of time, you'll build incredible momentum.

Everyone's home varies in size and severity of clutter, so give yourself a break and respect your own pace. You may need to break up each step into multiple work sessions. Once you get the hang of the process, you'll be able to apply this methodology to anything from a dresser drawer to an overflowing garage. Plan for longer work sessions (multiple hours or even a full day) as you learn the process and it becomes second nature to you. Include a partner or enlist your most focused friend(s) to help you stay on track.

PRO TIP: Set a timer for your allotted work time. This will give you a sense of how long these projects take. Use that insight to track and plan for future projects.

MEDITATE ON THIS

I want you to use this book as a guide. It's designed so it can be used across one intentional "Year of Clear," with projects broken down into weekly steps. I also realize that each of us has a different home, with different spaces, so use the book as a reference and choose your own adventure. The same method applies if your goal is to merely conquer that one disorganized drawer that drives you mad. Give yourself grace and apply the Simply Spaced method to any size project you want to tackle. My method is not intended to be dogma, but rather a helpful process so that you can start to think like an organizer about the systems and energy of your home.

A NOTE ON CO-HABITATION

This book is designed to be a guide for everyone in any living situation. It's important before you start this process to create some awareness around who you want to involve in your journey and how.

Live alone?

Congratulations! You already have everyone on board. Skip to Determine Your Clutter Capacity on page 18.

Live with roommates?

What's your relationship like? Have you lived together for years and plan on continuing to live together well into the future? Do you feel like family? If so, everything in the Live with Family section below will apply to you.

Not BFFs with your roomie?

Continue your journey without expectations that he or she will be participating. Some of the tips in the Live with Family section may help you think about how to do this.

Live with family?

A couple's therapist once told my husband and me early on in our relationship that we needed to figure out how to respect each other at home before we could respect each other out in the world. She asked us to close our eyes and imagine how we wanted our home to look, feel, and even smell. Happiness for me was a made bed, a tidy closet, and a candle burning. Happiness for my husband was watching a basketball game and screaming at the TV as if the players can actually hear him and he's part of the team...which he's not. And yet, here we were, sharing the same space every day. It's all about gentle compromise and mutual respect. When one person wants to get organized and another doesn't come around to it, there's a disconnect. We cannot force a certain type of order on one another. For one person, order may mean all the clothes in the closet are perfectly hung and color coded (me). For another, being organized simply means things are off the ground (my partner). Remember, it's all about compromise.

First, tell everyone what he or she needs to do to contribute to a harmonious, organized living arrangement. If you have children, consider their ages and set realistic expectations. A family can strengthen their connection through this process by understanding each other's individual needs, interests, and capacity to organize. Maintaining the systems that you set up may require some family "training." But I assure you, old dogs can be taught new tricks—and using clear labels keeps everyone on the same page. Whether you have a family or roomies, I recommend bringing them into the process as much as possible. You can even schedule "declutter" dates and set aside time to work together. If you're taking on decluttering sessions alone, be mindful when you come across items that don't belong to you. Making decisions about someone else's stuff is a slippery slope that could lead to anger or resentment if an item, especially something with sentimental value, is tossed. Instead, start an "Ask Johnny" bin to have him sort through later. I often work with one partner or family member and simply set aside anything questionable for others to look through when they can.

This is me, losing the battle of no TV in the bedroom, but my husband Jeff got a shoe tower, @ladyfierson will reign as the ultimate Netflix dog, and I hired a housekeeper to tame the traveling campsite. All is well in the world (until Jeff orders another pair of Off-Whites, of course).

Determine Your Clutter Capacity

Take the test below as an exercise in understanding how you work and live at home. What is your clutter capacity and what is the clutter capacity of those you live with? This awareness will help you communicate your needs to your co-habitants, make better judgments about what help you will need, and shed some light on the differences that keep you feeling at odds.

This best describes how I operate in my house:

A. I gravitate towards meticulously curated spaces.

B. I like a clean house, but I am okay with neat piles.

C. Too many systems make me anxious.

When guests are coming over:

A. I always arrange for the housekeeper to come clean first (you may be the housekeeper).

B. I can't wait to connect with friends and just throw my mess in a closet before they arrive.

C. I am watching TV until they ring the bell.

When I walk in the front door:

A. A clean house gives me an incredible sense of ease and calm.

B. My neat piles make me feel like everything's okay.

C. I'm just happy to be home, whether it's squeaky clean or covered in clutter.

I'm moving into a new house in a month:

A. I started decluttering a month ago, and I'm almost halfway packed.

B. I've thought about the organizing I plan to do before the movers come.

C. Let's make it easy and throw everything in a box.

My feelings about cleaning are:

A. I love it. It's cathartic. I'm a clean-as-you-go type.

B. With the right playlist and a glass of wine, I can get it done.

C. A little dirt and clutter never hurt anyone.

Mostly As: Gold
You are a Type A person and tidying up is your love language. You thrive in an environment that is clean, orderly, and systematic and get anxious when your organizational systems fall apart. It's important to understand this about yourself and explain your clutter personality type to the people you live with. Unless you live with other Golds, your home will never be exactly what you'd love it to be. So, consider getting extra help from outside the house, outsource and delegate tasks so you don't end up taking on too much or ending up resentful. You'll likely own the organizational management so start thinking like a boss (not to be confused with bossy).

Mostly Bs: Silver
You prefer an environment that is tidy and systematic but you're okay with "good enough." While relaxing on the couch, you're probably thinking about the clutter you shoved in the closet. Conflict will likely arise when you live with other silvers because you'll likely disagree about what you should focus on.

Mostly Cs: Bronze
You like to spread out and you're unfazed when things are scattered. You can step over a mess for weeks before it even catches your eye. You probably didn't even buy this book, but you took this quiz because a Gold or Silver you live with forced you to.

SUMMARY

Now that you've identified what organizational style is innate to each person in your house, how can this information help you? It's an opportunity for you to be more aware of each person's ability to participate in the process. By assessing your clutter capacity and that of the people around you, you can hone in on what's realistic for your household and make better decisions to support all parties involved. I first discovered this framework in a NAPO meeting taught by Wei Houng, CEO and Founder of The 6 Figure Academy. He laid out this simple concept as a way for organizers to better understand our clients. It was a game changer for me.

When I realized I was a Gold, living with two Bronze family members, I could finally forgive myself for not having it all together, all the time. It was a huge sense of relief because I had always felt like I was failing at home. Even as an organizer, my house didn't look perfect all the time. I found compassion for myself because, at the end of the day, I live with two people who don't prioritize or value neatness like I do. That awareness was an opportunity to implement systems that set me up for success. Now, we compromise by bringing in my team to organize a few times a month, and I hire a cleaning service to get us back to baseline every other week. If you are a Gold or Silver like me who lives with a Bronze (or many), and you constantly feel overwhelmed, rather than taking on the entire domestic load you may need to implement systems (like hiring a housekeeper or professional organizer) to find your peace.

THE METHOD

3 steps to transform your home and life.

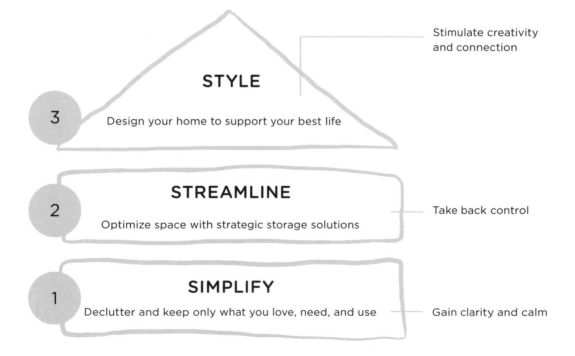

STYLE

3 — Design your home to support your best life

Stimulate creativity and connection

STREAMLINE

2 — Optimize space with strategic storage solutions

Take back control

SIMPLIFY

1 — Declutter and keep only what you love, need, and use

Gain clarity and calm

CHAPTER 1

KITCHEN

The kitchen is the epicenter of well-being in the home and a great place to start your organizational journey. An organized kitchen sets the tone for a harmonious home and is one that is free of clutter, has a spot for everything, and can inspire the preparation of healthy, stress-free meals. Whether you're a creative culinarian or delivery die-hard, a streamlined kitchen can foster efficiency while optimizing the function of your mind and body.

To be perfectly honest, I am not much of a cook, but my husband is. My mom, who's been living with us, also loves to cook and improvise. My husband spreads out and makes a mess while my mom loves to collect empty jars and leave a trail of them around the kitchen. I laugh and cry every time I walk in and see every drawer and cabinet remain open well after each meal. Because I have set up the kitchen in such a way that they can find everything—and I can put things away easily—we remain relatively organized. I set up systems when no systems existed, and I was able to organize the kitchen the way *they* need to use it and the way *I* need to be able to find things.

More than any other space, the kitchen demands efficiency, which is why it is imperative that you have a home for everything, as well as collaboration and everyone on board.

TOP CLUTTER CULPRITS

The kitchen is a notorious magnet for clutter, grime, and confusion, but I've heard many clients say that if they can keep their kitchen under control, they *feel* in control, even when the rest of the house seems chaotic. To take back the reins on the kitchen and curb the chaos, I've identified five common clutter culprits with five easy solutions:

Congregation gridlock
The kitchen is the high-traffic zone of the home. The more often it's used, the more likely there's disorder and mess. From kids' art corners to entire "office" workspaces, a kitchen can easily become the landing spot for more than just meals. Keep your family's health goals and special needs in mind while decluttering and organizing this space.

> **PRO TIP:** Move out anything that does not align with your family's goals for this space. It can be food that no longer serves you or broken dishes you've been meaning to replace.

System failure

"A place for everything, and everything in its place." Nowhere is this adage more important than in the kitchen. Without adequate space, proper storage, and identifiable zones, the kitchen becomes a free-for-all.

PRO TIP: Label zones that work and embrace the power of labels to maintain your working systems.

Perishable turnover

The kitchen is in constant flux like no other area of the home. Food flow changes daily, as do the tools and trials that accompany food prep.

PRO TIP: Keep your chalk or oil-based Sharpie pen in the kitchen and add "Opened On" dates to any perishable food.

The messiness of cooking

From meal prep to cooking and eating to cleanup, the kitchen is a mess magnet. Adopt a clean-as-you-go mentality for the kitchen and beyond. Don't let clutter build up to the point of feeling overwhelmed.

PRO TIP: Keep a bowl on the counter during food prep to toss all your excess, trash, or compostable items into.

Maintenance mishaps

One reason why our kitchens get out of control is due to a lack of maintenance. From regular cleanouts to cabinet overhauls, adopt healthy habits to keep clutter at bay.

PRO TIP: Schedule a bi-weekly or monthly clean out on your calendar or delegate this task.

GET MOTIVATED!

How do you keep yourself healthy? How do you nourish your family? The kitchen and its contents have the power to enrich your life's energy and support you in a thriving life. Most of us have health goals, and no matter where you are on that path, it helps both you and your family to be intentional about your use of this space. If your kitchen is out of control, this imbalance can affect many areas of your life.

For a kitchen that enhances your lifestyle, I advocate cultivating a clutter-free zone with intentional food systems. When nourishment is your central goal, cooking becomes more enjoyable and your home center is balanced. I believe that taking back control of the kitchen is an empowering first step in kick-starting your organizational journey.

SIMPLIFY: DECLUTTER YOUR CHAOTIC KITCHEN

The quickest way to regain control of your cluttered kitchen is to simplify. You can do this by discarding any items that are not in line with your current health, wellness, and lifestyle goals. It's easy to let things like junk mail, packages, and random clutter consume countertops and fill junk drawers. A total reset in this space will set you up with an intentional kitchen that will be easier to navigate.

Start decluttering with basic categories: Donate, Trash, and Recycle. Add additional categories as you move through the space, such as E-Waste, Other Rooms, and Return.

▷ **START HERE**

1. Complete worksheet 1 (on page 130)

Once you have completed the Pre-Worksheet on page 129 and before starting each step in this process, develop clear goals you have for your kitchen. Think about why you want to get this space organized and what it will feel like when you do. Complete the kitchen worksheet questions to define your "why" and to motivate and inform your decisions.

2. Set up your workspace

Use your standard tool kit as referenced on pages 9–10. Label your bins: Donate, Trash, Recycle, Other Room, and any additional categories that you'd like to consider.

COMMON KITCHEN AND PANTRY CATEGORIES

- Food:
  - Baking
  - Bread
  - Breakfast
  - Bulk or Backup
  - Cans
  - Coffee
  - Cooking
  - Condiments
  - Dairy
  - Drinks
  - Fruit
  - Grains

- Food:
  - Jars
  - Meat
  - Nuts
  - Dried Fruit
  - Oils & Vinegars
  - Pasta
  - School Snacks
  - Snacks
  - Spices
  - Superfoods
  - Sweets
  - Tea
  - Veggies

- Plates and Bowls
- Glasses
- Mugs
- Flatware
- Cutlery
- Pots and Pans (cookware)
- Bakeware
- Cooking Utensils
- Serving
- Party/ Entertainment
- BBQ
- Holiday
- Vases

- Candles
- Cookbooks
- Paper Goods
- Food Wrap / Storage Containers
- Cleaning
- First Aid

3. Pull everything out and group like-with-like

Begin in one area, drawer, or cabinet in your kitchen. Resist the urge to leave items in place or skip over "keep" items. There is power behind pulling everything out, and you are less likely to put back anything you don't love, need, or use. There is no hard rule for where to begin, but it is critical to take the time and energy necessary to address each item in your kitchen, from sink to stove.

> **PRO TIP:** If you are unable to tackle the whole kitchen at once, start with a cupboard, pantry, or one pre-categorized group like spices, pots, or pans.

4. Process your items

Donate, trash, or recycle any kitchen items that no longer serve a purpose. By purging unused appliances, tossing expired food, and streamlining collections of dishes to include only the most frequently used, you will see the room become more spacious and easier to navigate.

5. Wrap up

Always allow at least one hour for this step. Once you have processed your items, wrap up your work session by clearing away any trash, recycling, and donations from your kitchen. Put away all "Other Room" items around the house. If you are ready to move on, skip ahead to Streamline or put away any items that have an intuitive home and make note of any items that don't. Move any homeless items to a temporary landing zone.

> **PRO TIP:** This is a great time to do a deep clean, wipe down surfaces, or line shelving in your kitchen. Then take a deep breath and enjoy the cleared energy of your decluttered kitchen.

I love a well-curated, eclectic collection of items, but if you want to reduce visual clutter, streamline your basics. Uniform, cohesive collections are calming and clutter free. If replacing an item or group of items is in your budget, it's okay to let go of your mismatched or broken items. Make a note of anything you'd like to replace in your notebook.

MEDITATE ON THIS: TIME

It's totally normal if this process takes several work sessions to accomplish. Set another date with yourself, and perhaps an accountability buddy or partner, and then circle back to the top and start again.

15 THINGS TO LET GO OF NOW

1. Expired foods and spices

2. Foods misaligned with your current diet

3. Toxic and expired cleaning supplies

4. Mismatched/no-lid food storage containers

5. Appliances, dishes, and tools that are broken or missing parts

6. Gimmicky gadgets and impulse buys

7. Dud Duplicates (a fourth strainer with a broken handle, for example)

8. Reusable bag overflow

9. Outdated cookbooks and recipe cards

10. Unused china/crystal or your mother-in-law's fish plates (you can give them back)

11. Toxic, chemical-releasing cookware such as Teflon

12. Expired coupons, old receipts, menus, and manuals you can find online

13. Junk-drawer overflow: excess rubber bands, twist ties, corks, caps, and packaged condiments

14. Single-use disposables such as paper plates and plastic utensils

15. Overthinking

STREAMLINE: OPTIMIZE SPACE IN YOUR KITCHEN

With the excess and overflow out of the way, you are now ready to set up your kitchen. The next step in optimizing and organizing this space is to create homes for everything you've decided to keep.

▷ **START HERE**

1. Complete worksheet 2 (on page 131)

Use your worksheet to guide you through this process to refine your kitchen ecosystem. Identify what has and has not been working. Now that you have decluttered and identified your categories, think about what can be improved by optimizing storage.

2. Create zones

To figure out where to place items, match your Post-its from your categorized piles, place them in their optimal new homes, and then step back to consider how it all flows together. Store items where they are used. For instance, place a Post-it that says "Mugs and Glasses" on a cabinet near the refrigerator and coffee maker. By using Post-its, you'll be able to plan out the space without moving a single fork or spoon.

> **PRO TIP:** Identify and cull your everyday items. You can break the rule of "group like-with-like," but *only* if it makes sense to keep certain everyday items accessible. Limit yourself to a counter-top container or hanging utensil holder to store cooking essentials and everyday tools.

3. Maximize space

Adjust shelving, add pull-out drawers, and identify where you need storage solutions like shelf risers and drawer organizers. Use your walls and vertical space and take notes on any product solutions you may need in your worksheets. Visit simplyspaced.com/shop for our best clutter-free product recommendations.

> **PRO TIP:** Take measurements of drawers and cabinets and any space that needs storage. Hire a handyperson if you need an extra shelf or if you could benefit from pull-out drawers.

4. Implement storage solutions

For this step, it really helps to work with a blank canvas. Add in your shelf risers, storage baskets, lazy Susans, and whatever products will help optimize your space. Make sure everything fits to accommodate every category you need to store in your kitchen.

> **PRO TIP:** Determine placement of your storage solutions first, and then place everything that needs to live in the space.

Bamboo drawer organizers are a great solution for sustainable order in the kitchen.

Clear labels make everything immediately identifiable.

5. Label

One of the best ways to maintain an organized kitchen, or any space for that matter, is to use labels to help you and your loved ones remember where everything lives. Even temporary labels can go a long way until you and your family get used to the new system. If everything is clearly labeled and easy to see, it's more likely that everyone who uses your space will be on board with the changes.

PRO TIP: Test out your system. Once everything is put away in its new home, make sure the placement of items makes sense for you and others in your home. Sometimes a little trial and error is required before everything feels just right.

To set up my home pantry, I inventoried all the food categories that we always have on hand. The following list is how I have it divided:

- Backup
- Baking
- Bread
- Breakfast (cereal, oatmeal, granola)
- Cans
- Grains
- Jars
- Nuts
- Oils and Vinegars
- Pasta
- Savory Condiments
- Snacks
- Superfoods
- Sweet Condiments
- Sweets
- Tea/Coffee

Create stations based on common kitchen activities. If you make the same smoothie every morning, perhaps create a smoothie station with your blender and ingredients stored in the same cabinet. If you're an at-home barista, create a coffee station complete with hanging mugs for a fun-and-easy morning routine.

DIY ALL-PURPOSE CLEANER

Here's my favorite, quick, and not-so-dirty DIY recipe for a yummy scented all-purpose cleanser that I use all around my house, courtesy of my friend Larkin from Unfettered Home.

Time:
3 minutes

Makes:
One 16-ounce (473 ml) bottle of all-purpose cleaner

Ingredients:

- 1 teaspoon borax*
- ½ teaspoon washing soda* or baking soda
- 2 cups (473 ml) warm water
- 2 tablespoons (36 ml) liquid castile or dish soap
- 20 drops essential oil

Borax and washing soda can be found in most grocery and hardware stores.

Equipment:

- Spray bottle
- Funnel

Directions:

1. Fill spray bottle with dry ingredients first, followed by warm water, soap, and essential oil.

2. Swirl to combine ingredients completely before the first spray.

3. Enjoy less cleaning clutter and toxin-free peace of mind.

NOTE: Substitute dish soap with water and vinegar for a bare-bones version.

PRO TIP: Essential oils have antimicrobial properties and make your toxin-free cleaner smell great. Here are a few of my favorites:

Lavender = Relaxing
Tea Tree = Antimicrobial
Lemon = Uplifting and Degreasing
Orange = Purifying, Uplifting, and Degreasing
Thyme = Antimicrobial and goes perfectly with orange oil

STYLE: CURATE A KITCHEN THAT'S THE HEART OF YOUR HOME

A kitchen needs to be functional, but it can also be a place to inspire, nourish, and energize you. The last step in the organizing process is styling your space to reflect *you*, your goals, and the life you want to live. There is a different energy in a decluttered and intentionally styled kitchen that is joyful. You can find that delicate sweet spot by implementing a few simple styling hacks. Don't forget to make it fun!

▷ **START HERE**

1. Complete worksheet 3 (on page 132)
Use your worksheet to inspire some fresh styling elements in your newly organized kitchen. What will make you feel excited and encouraged to be in this space? Use the styling tips below, or any throughout the book, to style your space and make it your own.

2. Curate your counters
I talked about keeping your everyday tools and utensils accessible, so perhaps this is a good opportunity to find a beautiful vessel or heirloom that can double as a utilitarian home. If your counters now only house appliances you use every day, they will look less cluttered. Instead, display a few of your favorite cookbooks or put a decorative cutting board or candle on the counter. Small, personal touches like these add a sense of warmth and give the space a less sterile look while maintaining the order you've been craving.

3. Add hooks and hanging shelves
Whether you are hanging kitchen towels or drying chilis, kitchen hooks and hanging shelves are some of the most functional and stylish additions you can add to your space. Don't be afraid to add some of your own flair, such as a beautiful apron, a favorite farmers' market bag, or a Turkish hand towel. Stylish storage is my secret weapon for small spaces.

Adding floating shelves, hooks, and a vertical wall grid created a beautiful and functional vignette in this kitchen. Clear glass and BPA-free containers keep dry goods looking chic and fresh, while an oil painting and greenery bring life to this side of the kitchen.

4. Master the art of decanting

One of my favorite tips for a tidy kitchen lies in the decanting method. Today, so much of what we buy comes in packages that function mostly as advertising. Take items like liquid soap, nuts, seeds, and supplements—even flour and baking items—out of their plastic packaging and display them in transparent glass jars to give your space a magazine-ready feel that's functional (and healthier than plastics). Decanting allows you to see what you have, saves space, and reduces advertising, plastics, and cardboard. Plus, it looks beautiful! If you are in the "life's too short to decant your cornflakes" camp, own it and stick to styling with what you love and use.

> **PRO TIP:** Buy in bulk to reduce packaging and write details and expiration dates on the bottom of items with a white paint marker or Sharpie, which can be easily removed from glass with rubbing alcohol.

Take items out of their original excess packaging and store them in streamlined bins, jars, baskets, etc. to maximize space and maintain freshness.

5. Identify your top three

In any space in your home, identify the three most significant decorative items that you'd like to feature. You may have more than three, but choose and name only three to start. Maybe you have a favorite painting, a handmade ceramic bowl, or a fancy teapot. Let those items shine and decorate your kitchen with a personal touch.

You can mix materials, but keep your heavier, darker items to the bottom and lighter, transparent items to the top.

Styling your favorite kitchen items is a great way to break from the rigidity of a like-with-like system. If you love it and use it, display it.

CHAPTER 2

BEDROOM

If the kitchen is the epicenter of well-being for our health, then the bedroom is the epicenter of well-being for our relationships, including our relationship to ourselves. How much sleep are you getting? How much do you want to get? What's keeping you up at night? Do you step into your closet and walk out feeling empowered or beleaguered? Everything we do during the day starts and stops at the bedroom door, so keeping this space calm and clutter-free is paramount.

For me, the bedroom is the place I go at the end of the day to unwind, reenergize, and connect with my husband. I've made it a clutter-free zone by organizing it in a way that works for both of us. My husband knows I love sleep more than anything, and I have a hard time falling asleep if this space is in disarray. In fact, the physical act of "tidying up" is my love language. When my husband keeps our bedroom clean, he is expressing his love for me in a way that fills my love tank. I mention this difference because it's important to understand what our partners need to feel loved, which often doesn't match what we need. When it comes to our bedroom, my husband Jeff keeps it neat not because it matters to him, but because he understands my values and what makes me happy. Revisit the cohabitation section on page 17 and Determine Your Clutter Capacity on page 18 to find out your clutter color. To take the test online, head over to simplyspaced.com/cluttercapacity now.

TOP CLUTTER CULPRITS

The bedroom is a place for rest and relaxation, but when clutter creeps in it's hard to slow down and enjoy it. But what if your bedroom could feel rejuvenating? What if you could keep it clutter free and restful? To get your bedroom back to basics, I've identified five common clutter culprits with five tips to implement now:

Clothes here, there, and everywhere

A solid 80 percent of bedroom clutter is clothing related. Start by placing all your stray clothes into the laundry or closet. I'll talk about clothing in the next chapter. If clothes are your biggest challenge, you may want to start there, but this is an exercise in seeing your room as it is meant to be. Once you clear out clothes clutter, you'll experience an immediate shift in your space. As I dial in on the purpose of this room, you'll be able to see and appreciate its potential and be more inclined to keep clothes relegated to their real homes: the closet, dresser, and maybe even some wall hooks.

> **PRO TIP:** Purchase a divided laundry hamper to keep clothing piles off the floor. I use mine for darks, whites, and specialty cleaning.

Messy bed

Most of us have heard the productivity hack that a made bed in the morning can set the tone for the rest of the day. But what most of us don't realize is that a messy bed can make the entire room feel disorganized even if it isn't. An unmade bed is also a temptation to go back to sleep. Sometimes completing the simplest task can help clear your mind and make you feel more in control.

PRO TIP: Make your bed every day to instantly make your room look less cluttered and to gain back control of this space and your day.

The traveling campsite

One of my favorite movies as a kid was *The Neverending Story*. For those of you not familiar with this movie, there's this evil that's taking over a magical land called "The Nothing." It's threatening to swallow the magical land whole. Well, The Nothing is basically my husband's traveling campsite, which consists of anything from dirty dishes to yesterday's socks. It goes with him anywhere he goes and if left unchecked, could swallow our home up whole, like The Nothing.

PRO TIP: Designate a storage bin or basket that can serve as a catch-all for clutter. This basket can be moved around the house as the receptacle for putting away miscellaneous objects. It's also acceptable to assign this task to someone else or make it a fun game.

Open storage

I know what you're thinking—easy access, right? Not quite. Open shelves and wide, flat surfaces attract clutter. Cluttered walls and overflowing shelves can make you feel stressed—not relaxed—before bed.

PRO TIP: Consider replacing open shelving with dressers and closed storage in the bedroom to reduce visual chaos (and get a better night's sleep).

Multi-use space

Maybe you live in a small city apartment, a house with a bunch of roommates, or perhaps your own studio. Regardless of your living situation, I want you to think of your bedroom as a sacred space and omit as many distractions as possible. That means stop paying your bills (or eating!) in bed.

PRO TIP: Remove any items or projects that don't have to do with your intentions for the bedroom, including paperwork, bills, video games, and if your partner agrees, that flat screen TV.

GET MOTIVATED!

Commit to making your bedroom a sanctuary that supports the goals you have for yourself or your relationship. Eliminating clutter in the bedroom will represent the clearing of the past and commitment to your current life. If you are looking to reconnect with your partner, don't neglect it. Nurturing your relationship and honoring your sleep is an important part of a healthy lifestyle. Look for beauty in the simplicity.

Designate a catch-all basket that can be moved from room to room to put things away.

SIMPLIFY: DECLUTTER YOUR BUSY BEDROOM

Just like we did in the kitchen, this project will involve touching every item in your bedroom, identifying if it is something you love, need, or use, and most importantly asking yourself: does this support my intentions for this space?

▷ START HERE

1. Complete worksheet 1 (on page 133)
Before starting each step in this process, identify the goals you have for your bedroom. Think about why you want to get this space organized and what it will feel like when you do. Complete the worksheet questions for an exercise in defining your "why" and to motivate and inform your decisions.

2. Set up your workspace
Use your standard tool kit as referenced on pages 9-10. Label your bins: Donate, Trash, Recycle, Other Room, and any additional categories that you'd like to consider.

> **PRO TIP:** Pick up all the clothes hung over chairs or tossed in piles, so you can organize all clothing at once. Move these items to the laundry room or closet so all your clothes are in one place. If clothes are your biggest problem area, you have the option to skip to the next chapter and begin there.

3. Pull everything out and group like-with-like
As we've established, there is no one perfect place to start, but working clockwise through the room and focusing on visible clutter is a good starting point. Touch every item, pull it out, and create categories for each thing you come across. Use the listed categories for reference and subcategorize as categories grow. When you have more than two pieces of bedding, you can start to divide that section into sub-categories: pillows, sheets, blankets, etc. If you have seven different types of sheets, divide the sheets by type: top sheets, fitted sheets, and so on.

4. Process your items
Donate, trash, or recycle any bedroom item that you do not love, need, or use. The key to a successful bedroom declutter is a commitment to removing any items that do not need to live here anymore. Remember, there is energy in every item you own. There are subliminal messages being sent to you and to your partner all the time. What books do you keep by your nightstand? What rituals have you brought to the bedroom that would be better suited for the garage? Be intentional about what you choose to keep.

> **MEDITATE ON THIS:**
> **THE POWER OF POST-ITS**
>
> Still using your Post-its? I promise it will help keep you from getting overwhelmed, because before you know it, you'll have things everywhere. This will also help anyone who comes in to see the method of your madness rather than just a giant mess. Post-its are a simple, low-tech way to organize, and they are surprisingly powerful for encouraging action. Don't skip this step!

5. Wrap up
Always allow at least one hour for this step. Once you have processed your items, wrap up your work session by clearing away any trash, recycling, and donations from your bedroom. Put away all "Other Room" items in locations around the house. If you are ready to move on, skip ahead to step 2, Streamline, or put away any items that have an intuitive home and take notes in your notebook about any items that don't. Move any homeless items to a temporary landing zone.

> **PRO TIP:** This is a great time to practice the habit of making your bed so that your bedroom instantly looks tidy and put together. Take a deep breath and enjoy the cleared energy of your decluttered bedroom.

Donate items that you no longer love, need, or use.

15 THINGS TO LET GO OF NOW

1. Expired products
2. Used candles
3. Books that are not in alignment with your goals
4. Magazines that you'll never read
5. Keepsakes you don't love
6. Outdated tech (especially bad energy for the bedroom)
7. Old or expired medications and prescriptions
8. Dry-cleaning bags
9. Unused suitcases
10. Stained, torn, or worn linens
11. Old glasses
12. Pillows over two years old
13. Paid bills, receipts, and paper*
14. Tattered clothing*
15. Blame

Refer to the corresponding chapter

COMMON BEDROOM CATEGORIES

- Accessories
  - Hats
  - Jewelry
  - Sunglasses
- Bedding
  - Blankets
  - Pillows
  - Sheets
- Throws
- Beauty*
- Books
- Clothing*
- Decor
- Electronics
- Exercise Equipment
- Garment Bags
- Grooming
- Magazines
- Mementos*
- Paper*
- Sewing
- Shoes*
- Toys

Refer to the corresponding chapter

STREAMLINE: OPTIMIZE SPACE IN YOUR BEDROOM

Once you've decluttered your bedroom by removing anything that does not support your goals for the space, it's time to think about optimal storage solutions. Remember, I'm not talking about styling, or folding clothes, or even the best record to play on the record player you just found. It's time to start thinking about zones and storage. If you've used temporary solutions to store items neatly in your space, think about what permanent solutions can be used to maximize space.

3. Maximize space

Think outside the box. How can you be creative and make better use of your space? Since the bed takes up so much horizontal space in most bedrooms, it's critical to maximize usable space, without overpowering the walls. Could you use vertical walls in narrow corners and empty wall space for hanging hats? Guitars? Art or photos, mirrors, or even love notes? You could even use hooks on empty walls, behind doors, or on the wall to the master bathroom. Maximize the space under the bed with pullout bins and baskets. This underutilized space is great for extra bedding and even those pillows you love to style but never use.

PRO TIP: Keep clothes off the ground by adding hooks or baskets where dirty clothing can land.

▷ **START HERE**

1. Complete worksheet 2 (on page 134)

Use your worksheet to guide you through this process to refine your bedroom ecosystem. Identify what has and has not been working. Now that you have decluttered and identified your categories, think about what can be improved by optimizing storage.

2. Create zones

Make a list of all the categories you've identified in your bedroom and use your sticky notes to identify the optimal zones for each. Place the Post-its in areas of the room where it would make sense to collect your items. Do you want to keep all beauty items together near a vanity or relocate them to the bathroom? Assign zones to each category based on where you're most likely to need them. Repurpose shoe boxes, baskets, or baggies to corral items if you do not have the perfect storage solution yet. Take notes on any products, storage solutions, or furniture you'll need to maximize your space.

4. Implement storage solutions

Whether it's wall shelves or drawer dividers, baskets for your nightstand or rolling racks for under the bed, a few key storage solutions can help you maintain a clutter-free bedroom with ease.

5. Label

Labels in the bedroom can be a game changer, not just for clothing and dressers, but also for those hard-to-reach spaces like high shelves, under-bed pullouts, or concealed storage.

STYLE: CURATE YOUR BEDROOM TO REFLECT YOU, YOUR PARTNER, AND YOUR GOALS

First and foremost, the bedroom is designed for sleep, one of the most important functions in our lives. Crisp, clean, comfortable linens make for an immediate room transformation, while the addition of a cozy throw or a few stylish pillows can pull together plain bedding. Styling your bedroom can be an opportunity to celebrate and honor you and your partner—or a way to set an intention for the partnership you wish to enter. So often, this space, rarely seen by the rest of the world, is the last one we think to style. But considering we sleep for a good third of our lives, it's important to cultivate this space with love.

▷ START HERE

1. Complete worksheet 3 (on page 135)
Use your worksheet to inspire some fresh styling elements in your newly organized bedroom. What will make you feel excited and encouraged to be in this space? Use the tips below, or any throughout the book, to style your space and make it your own.

2. Showcase your favorites
In the bedroom—the doorway to our day—it's important to highlight special items that inspire you and make you feel good. Think about a quote you'd like to wake up to every morning or that pair of shoes you worked to buy. Put the possessions and treasures that bring you joy on display. Create and style those favorite items into vignettes using trays, mirrors, or books. You can let your intuition be your guide or follow the styling tips throughout this book to develop a knack for curating a space you love.

There's nothing like fresh flowers to brighten up a bedroom with an instant boost.

Arrange your favorite items into vignettes.

Trays neatly organize small trinkets.

6. Layer your bed like a pro

A beautiful bed ties the room together as the focal point, so investing in beautiful bedding will instantly make your room shine. Use large Euro pillows to add height to the back of your bed or a set of two side-by-side pillows against the headboard, adorned with two more pillows in front of them. Turn down a quilt or blanket over your duvet to add texture. Or fold your duvet or blanket at the foot of the bed. I like to keep my bedding neutral, but I add dimension by mixing materials and textures like cotton, linen, and velvet. Add small pillows and a throw in a new pattern or material.

PRO TIP: Use a duvet or down pillows one size too big for their covers for a luxe, plush look.

3. Display with a tray

One of the best ways to keep your bedroom tidy is to use trays to corral all the trinkets and small objects that collect in this space. From keys and cufflinks to glasses and aspirin, a nightstand tray can be a stylish multi-purpose organizing tool.

4. Curate a gallery wall

The bedroom is a great place to feature important sentimental objects like that matchbook from your first date or family heirlooms. You can frame or hang almost anything, so think about the most precious items that represent the ones you love and celebrate them in your most sacred space.

5. Rekindle the romance

When it comes to styling a bedroom, try a few of my favorite things to transform your space into that romantic notions mecca: plants, candles, flowers, and books. Each brings instant warmth, energy, and style with minimal effort.

CHAPTER 3

CLOSET

In 2017, I worked with a professional organizer and stylist, my friend Shira Gill, to help me declutter my own closet. I thought to myself, "I'm an organizer. So, why am I having such a hard time getting through my own closet clutter?" Then I realized that I hadn't yet figured out my own self-sabotaging beliefs around clothes.

The truth is, while I lead my clients through this powerful process day-in and day-out, like most of us, it's always harder to look in the mirror at ourselves and our own habits. It wasn't until I truly surrendered to the process myself that I started to rethink my own values, goals, and the way I show up in the world with my wardrobe. Before I organized my closet with intention, I felt overwhelmed most mornings, scrambling to put something together and not feeling my best for the rest of the day.

Why? Because like many of the clients I work with, I put myself last most of the time. Coming out of a career in film production, my closet reflected my top priorities: comfort first, simplicity second, and style only on occasion. But I felt like I had come a long way from the days of paint-splattered jeans and Converse sneakers ("the official production uniform" as my husband deemed it), and I wanted my closet to reflect my transformation. It wasn't until I had a friend call me out on my "go-to" leggings and tees that I started to see how I was showing up.

Shira challenged me to think about the boss I wanted to be and the ways I could shift my mindset to dress the way I wanted to feel. She reminded me that it's about aspirations, goals, and curating the version of yourself you *want* to become, even if you aren't quite there yet. Shira helped me toss the tattered and out-of-style, the duds, the dreary, and the juvenile. We noted a few missing pieces that would pull me out of the past and into the present, but it was mostly about letting go.

By getting rid of what no longer served me, I was able to see the pieces I loved, because they were no longer hidden behind the excess. I realized that without buying anything, I already had amazing clothes in my closet. I now intentionally keep my closet minimal, so I never have to feel overwhelmed. I buy staple, quality, well-made pieces and create outfits that I know work together. I can find and pair clothes easily, and everything I own feels intentional. Most importantly, I feel empowered throughout my day. It all starts first thing in the morning when I put on my clothes. An organized, intentional closet has been such a game-changer for me, one that I wish for you as I share some tips to help you along your journey. Remember, less is more. Start by decluttering your closet, and you just may be surprised at what you find.

TOP CLUTTER CULPRITS

Closets are a major pain point for many of us because while clothing selection in stores and online is limitless, our closets can only hold so much. Most people aren't thinking about why they

shop or where their items will be stored, but rather about the feel-good, quick fix of a shopping spree. Unfortunately, that mindset is a recipe for closet disaster. Here are five common clutter culprits with five easy tips to take back control of the clothing chaos:

Too much in, too little out

One of the main causes of closet clutter is the constant influx with no editing. We live in a fast fashion world where we can buy clothes quick and cheap, and it's easy to accumulate them. Without a radical edit or shift in perspective and new habits, clothing clutter is inevitable.

PRO TIP: Forget the fads and stick to quality basics. Adopt a one-in, one-out policy, replacing throwaway trends with quality classics that will stand the test of time.

Hanger hoarding

From wire dry-cleaning hangers to mismatched hangers of all shapes and sizes, this is one item we all struggle to let go of. Hangers clutter our floors, rods, and closets—taking up unnecessary space and ruining clothes.

PRO TIP: Replace your hangers with one streamlined hanger type. Get rid of dry-cleaning hangers and plastic immediately—or even better, bring your own hangers to the cleaners.

Sluggish storage

We want to believe that if we just get rid of the excess we'll magically be organized, but sometimes, all you need is a container.

PRO TIP: A rolling cart for shoes, a good old-fashioned hat bin, or a set of wall hooks for belts will get you organized.

MEDITATE ON THIS: THE CAPSULE WARDROBE

Decision fatigue is real. We have too many choices, and it begins at the closet door. This is why I am blown away by the new trends in minimalist fashion, advances in sustainable clothing, and growing interest in capsule collections. The demand is shifting to wearable, interchangeable clothes that pair well rather than one-offs that lose their charm after one wear.

It's my mission to make this more than a trend, but a lifestyle. I see clients get more excited about what they can get rid of than what they can consume. Shopper's high has transformed into giver's high as we embrace the "less is more" lifestyle. We want less stuff; we want to be able to find things easily; and we want it to look great. Quality over quantity is the answer to making this vision a sustainable reality. Change how you show up in the world!

By removing anything that I don't love, need, or wear, and by intentionally curating my closet, I feel less stressed and more empowered in the mornings.

Poor use of space

Our closets are filled with every style of clothing, fabric, and color, and a simple rod on the wall just won't cut it anymore. You need adequate storage to accommodate a variety of clothing options.

> **PRO TIP:** Ditch the rod and shelf and install a modular closet that will maximize space in your closet, no matter how big or small. With options galore—from stores like Ikea and The Container Store to Home Depot—the custom solutions are endless, easy, and affordable.

The sunk cost fallacy

You're thinking, "I spent good money on this shirt, so I have to keep it. Right?" This flawed thinking is what keeps so many of us buried in clutter and hanging onto items we will never wear.

> **PRO TIP:** Turn your clothes into cash through online consignment shops like thredUP or The RealReal; sell items on Poshmark or eBay; or drop your expensive goods off at a resale shop like Buffalo Exchange. Forget about the sunk cost and think about the cost of your sanity.

GET MOTIVATED!

When it comes to organizing your closet, it's important to think about how you want to look and feel. Are you currently stepping into a new career and want to feel like a total boss? Or are you ready to ditch the heels for a more laid-back, Southern California vibe? Maybe you just moved to NYC and you're ready to curate that capsule collection or you are a new mom with a new body. Whatever your intentions are for this process, bring your attention to the energy behind your decisions and come back to bigger goals of optimizing your home to support living your best life.

There's no better place than the closet to help us see our own reflection. If your home is a mirror for your life, your clothes are the projection screen of that image. What's the story that you're telling now? What is the story that you want to tell? Get rid of anything that doesn't align with where you are now in your life and where you are going. Use the worksheets at the back of this book to get started and be honest with yourself. Do these clothes make you feel empowered? Sure, you can ask them if they bring you joy, but is that all you're looking for? For me, I want to feel happy and energized when I get dressed, but I also want to feel strong, powerful, and above all else, confident.

SIMPLIFY: DECLUTTER YOUR CRAMMED CLOSET

As I've established, getting organized always starts with decluttering. I call this the Simplify step because once you remove the excess and identify the items you still love, need, and wear, getting dressed will be much simpler. This is a great exercise to do with a friend or your most trusted fashionista, but you are more than capable of doing this on your own. Keep only the things that are in alignment with your life now and in the near future.

▷ **START HERE**

1. Complete worksheet 1 (on page 136)

Before starting each step in this process, get clear on the goals you have for your closet. Think about why you want to get this space organized and what it will feel like when you do. How would it feel if you could find what you need? If you had outfits that worked together and clothes that made you look and feel the way you want to? Complete the worksheet questions for an exercise in defining your "why" and to motivate and inform your decisions.

2. Set up your workspace

Use your standard tool kit as referenced on pages 9–10. Label your bins: Donate, Trash, Recycle, Other Room, and any additional categories that you'd like to consider. Common ones are: Sell, Repair, Tailor, Dry Clean, and Give to Mom.

> **PRO TIP:** If your closet is adjacent to a bedroom, it's helpful to clear your room first so you can use the bed and floor space as you pull everything out.

3. Pull everything out and group like-with-like

Start in one area of your closet. When you pull everything out, you are less likely to put back something you no longer love, need, or use. Take out all your shoes and group them by category. When it comes to clothing, it's also helpful to sub-categorize by color to see how much you have of each type. How do you determine like-with-like? You can use the list at the end of this section or categorize by how you instinctively search for your clothes. Here are some options:

- Clothing Type
- Style
- Fit
- Color
- Brand
- Length
- Occasion
- Season
- Mood
- Capsule Collection

> **PRO TIP:** Use a rolling rack to sort your clothes as you pull them out of the closet. This will give you extra space to see everything that you own.

4. Process your items

The key to a successful closet declutter is a commitment to your overarching goals. If your goal is to get rid of excess, you will need to be diligent about only keeping the clothes that make you feel good and support the life you are living right now. Not every piece will bring you joy, and only some will still serve a purpose. But if you no longer love, need, or use it—lose it.

5. Wrap up

Always allow at least one hour for this step. Once you have processed your items, wrap up your work session by clearing away any trash, recycling, and donations from your closet or workspace. Put away all "Other Room" items in homes around the house. If you are ready to move on, skip ahead to step 2, Streamline, or put away any items that have an intuitive home and take notes in your notebook about any items that don't. Move any homeless items to a temporary landing zone.

> **PRO TIP:** Fix or repair any favorite but damaged items instead of replacing or donating them. It's a sustainable alternative to letting them go. But remember, keep only what you will repair. Take a deep breath and enjoy the cleared energy of your decluttered closet.

Group similar items or categories of items together based on item type or function.

15 THINGS TO LET GO OF NOW

1. Stained or destroyed clothes
2. Faded items (and not in that cool way)
3. Any uncomfortable clothes and shoes
4. Hand-me-downs you don't love
5. "Someday I'll lose the weight" clothes
6. High-maintenance items (things that take too much time to clean, iron, and fuss over)
7. Socks without a match
8. The jeans from when you were 19
9. Bras that don't fit
10. Jewelry and gifts from your ex
11. Broken jewelry
12. Costume jewelry (give it to your kids)
13. Hats with sweat stains
14. Wire hangers
15. Not enoughness

COMMON CLOTHING CATEGORIES

- Tops
  - Tanks/Strapless
  - Long Sleeve
  - Short Sleeve
- Bottoms
  - Pants/Jeans
  - Shorts
  - Skirts
  - Leggings
- Outerwear
  - Coats and Jackets
  - Cardigans
  - Sweaters
  - Hoodies
- Dresses/Jumpsuits
  - Shoes
  - Sandals
  - Flats
  - Boots
  - Heels
  - Sneakers
  - Slippers
- Accessories
  - Hats
  - Belts
  - Scarves
  - Purses
  - Wallets
- Winter Wear
  - Gloves
  - Hats
  - Scarves
- Suits
- Workout
- Undergarments
- Swim
- Bathrobes
- Costumes

STREAMLINE: OPTIMIZE SPACE IN YOUR CLOSET

If you can't find anything at home and there's clutter everywhere, it's going to affect your day-to-day flow. An organized closet with the right systems in place will make you feel in control and make every day so much easier. Follow the steps below to optimize space in your closet.

▷ **START HERE**

1. Complete worksheet 2 (on page 137)
Use your worksheet to guide you through this process to refine your closet. Identify what has and has not been working. Now that you have decluttered and identified your categories, think about what can be improved by optimizing storage.

2. Create zones
Make a list of all the categories you've created in your closet or wardrobe. Use your sticky notes to identify the optimal zones for each group based on ease of access. Identify and cull your regularly worn items. You can break the rule of like-with-like if it makes sense to keep certain items accessible.

> **PRO TIP:** Try incorporating seasonal rotations if you are short on space. Keep out-of-season clothing up high or in another area of the house.

3. Maximize space
Move shelves, identify areas where you could use a shelf riser, use your walls and vertical space, and take notes. Shoe shelves, pullouts, cohesive bins, and clutch organizers go a long way for increasing visibility. Jot down all the supplies or solutions you'll need to store and see everything in each zone. If you don't see it, you won't use it.

> **PRO TIP:** Add purse hangers to maximize space on existing rods.

Fabric-lined baskets are a favorite product for closets and a great way to keep out-of-sight storage contained and accessible. Just add labels.

Stacking shoe bins maximize space.

We used office file organizers to store clutches for our client to maximize space and keep her collection tidy.

4. Implement storage solutions

Whether it's an entirely new modular closet, a few shoe shelves, or baskets, bins, and belt racks, install your new systems yourself or bring in a handyperson. If your closet is small and you need additional dresser space, you can use drawer organizers to separate smaller items like undergarments and socks.

> **PRO TIP:** Store luxury, specialty, or sentimental pieces in archival boxes with acid-free tissue paper.

5. Label

One of the main reasons I use labels on drawers and in closets is to find things quickly. If anyone else is doing laundry, he or she will know where everything goes so I won't have to dig through my sock drawer to find my swimsuit.

> **PRO TIP:** Explain your new labeling system to your housekeeper, helpful mom, family members, or anyone else in your house who puts away the clothes.

Add drawer organizers to give structure, order, and a home for everything.

STYLE: CURATE YOUR CLOSET

It may not be intuitive to think about your closet as a place you need to style, but as someone who does this for a living, I can't tell you how powerful it is to see my clients' faces when we add a few elements that personalize their closets. The name of the game: less is more. It doesn't take a lot to transform a closet from just another utilitarian storage space to an inspiring boutique-like canvas that you can't wait to explore.

▷ START HERE

1. Complete worksheet 3 (on page 138)
Think about what you would love your closet to look and feel like. What are your goals for the look of this space, and what elements will make it feel inspiring? Answer the questions in your worksheet to get started.

2. Swap out your mismatched hangers
The number one way to instantly transform your closet is to use uniform hangers. Try slimline hangers if you have a lot of clothing and you're likely to shop before you edit. Slimline hangers are ideal for small closets and anywhere you are short on space. Opt for wooden hangers if you like a more curated look and you want to keep your collection minimal.

3. Pair ten outfits you love
Think about the types of events or occasions that you dress for. Make a list and put together ten go-to outfits that you can grab in a pinch.

PRO TIP: Try on your top ten outfits, take a photo on your phone, and start an "outfits" folder for inspiration. Send it to your fashion-forward friend for approval, if you need some guidance.

What is your hanger personality? I am wood, and my husband is slimline. Why? Because I'm very intentional about wanting a capsule collection and get overwhelmed by too many options. I like to curate things and my weight is relatively stable, so I prefer a wooden hanger.

4. Invest in your quality basics

Invest in a few, high-quality basics from each clothing category that will stand the test of time and look beautiful in your closet and on your body. Remember, being organized isn't just about getting rid of the old, but also about completing your look so you feel good about what you own. It takes a little pre-planning, but it's worthwhile to make the upfront investment.

PRO TIP: Commit to a brand or two that you absolutely love. Create a uniform out of their best basics and add in great shoes and accessories.

File-fold your clothes to the size of your drawers to see exactly what you have and to keep your clothing tidy.

Consider repurposing a cabinet with divided, labeled drawers to store overflow accessories and keep them organized. All my favorite products are listed on simplyspaced.com/shop

5. Create a display area

Dedicate a display area for your favorite items: sunglasses, perfume, earrings, go-to accessories, an inspirational image of your favorite icon.

PRO TIP: Show off those fancy shoes and purse boxes rather than tossing them. They can also be used as hidden storage or to prop-up your display.

6. File-fold

We all know about the art of the file-fold thanks to Marie Kondō, and we're keeping it up because it works and looks amazing.

PRO TIP: Fold to the size of your drawers so your clothing items stand up like a file. Fold clothes in halves or thirds depending on the depth of the drawer so you can see each item. Color code for bonus styling points if that's your jam.

CHAPTER 4

BATH AND BEAUTY

The bathroom is unequivocally my favorite space in the house. It's the one place where I can always unwind, and even when it's a mess, I can quickly get it back to baseline. Whether or not your bathroom is a spa-like dreamland like mine, it certainly has the potential to be. The truth is, there's nothing intrinsically special about it. It's only special because I intend it to be. Every day, at the end of a long organizing session, my favorite thing to do is take a hot bath with bath salts to ease my sore muscles. I read a book and light a candle. I never get sick of it.

I don't know if you've noticed, but we are in the middle of a self-care revolution, which comes as no surprise considering the frenetic world we live in. Sometimes the only time I have to myself is when I'm alone in my bathroom, which is why I am a huge advocate for reclaiming this space as a sanctuary for serenity, calm, and quiet. I've probably written half this book in the bathtub. Why? Because I can hardly hear my own thoughts anywhere else and have embraced the stillness as my own little corner of the world.

But I understand that it's no fun stepping over piles of towels, toys, and broken hair clippers to get there. You won't feel inspired if you're surrounded by mess. I believe that with a detox plus a few styling tips and tricks, you too can experience the spa-like experience I'm touting.

I organize garages, haul away clutter, and drive around LA looking for recycling bins and e-waste stations for a living. It's not glamorous, but I love my job. It's hard work, yet it's rewarding and fulfilling. I am exhausted by the end of my work day, but that's why I implore rituals to revive and revitalize my spirit daily. A bath, a nap, or a ten-minute meditation does the trick. I also try to take "mini-vacations" throughout my day that remind me I'm still human. Not taking time for ourselves can make us sick, cause us to make mistakes, and even get in car accidents (it's true!). The universe will continue to throw obstacles in your way until you learn a different way. So, it's time to slow down, prioritize, and declutter your life. Let's tackle the bathroom together.

TOP CLUTTER CULPRITS

If you ever feel like the harmony is lost in the rest of your house, try organizing your bathroom to make the sanctuary you always dreamed of. With a little self-love and intention, you can transform this space to make it your own. Here are five common clutter culprits and five tips to get started now:

Product overload

From hundreds of hair-care items and free samples to expired medications and empty containers, bathrooms are magnets for disorder. They are dumping grounds for a constant influx of pharmacy products and single-use items that are forgotten in hard-to-reach cabinets.

System failure

The problem with most bathrooms is a case of over-buying and under-utilization. Product piles are quick to build up, and a lack of storage makes it hard to find your belongings. You often end up buying more than you need and re-buying things you already own.

Too many towels

This is the one category even the most fastidious organizers who are adept at editing out unwanted or unused items tend to overlook. In truth, towels should be replaced every two years. Most people never replace them and have many more than they need.

Counter chaos

Counters collect all of our beauty and self-care products, and we tend to leave everything out in plain view due to improper storage and deep cabinets that are hard to access. Before we know it, we're faced with a mound of clutter.

Cabinet limitations

Most bathrooms don't have enough storage, so it's imperative to get creative.

GET MOTIVATED!

If a bathroom that doubles as a spa seems impossible but appealing, follow along with this chapter to simplify, streamline, and style your watery wonderland. It doesn't take much to transform this space, and clearing clutter is always the first step. When it comes to letting go, if you can't make an educated choice, make a conscious one. Let go of anything that won't enhance your life, from expired products to samples that are also wasteful and toxic. Remember, it's all about your overarching vision, and if your ultimate goal is to declutter and reduce overwhelm, get rid of the excess.

Define a maximum number of items for specific high-volume groupings. Once your maximum quantity is reached, it's time to edit.

SIMPLIFY: DECLUTTER YOUR BRIMMING BATHROOM

This project will involve pulling everything out of every drawer, cabinet, and hidden cavernous space. Identify if it is something you love, need, or use. Most importantly, ask yourself, "Is this something I would buy now? Do I need this? Is this expired, old, or toxic?" It's important to clean out your beauty products regularly because many of these items can become harmful if they are left in plastic and exposed to heat, which changes their chemical make-up.

START HERE

1. Complete worksheet 1 (on page 139)
Before starting each step in this process, identify the goals you have for your bathroom. Think about why you want to get this space organized and what it will feel like when you do. Complete the worksheet questions for an exercise in defining your "why" and to motivate and inform your decisions.

2. Set up your workspace
Use your standard tool kit as referenced on pages 9–10. Label your bins: Donate, Trash, Recycle, Other Room and any additional categories that you'd like to consider.

3. Pull everything out and group like-with-like
Begin in one area in your bathroom and pull everything out, grouping like-with-like. Use the category list included in this chapter to determine what categories of items you have.

4. Process your items
Donate, trash, or recycle any bathroom items that you do not love, need, or use. Set aside items that need to be recycled safely, like medications, needles, or expired hair dyes. Keep only the products that fit your current beauty or healthcare regimen.

My husband will attest to the fact that I love to zone out in the beauty aisle, but streamlining my grooming routine has been good for my body and wallet.

5. Wrap up

Always allow at least one hour for this step. Once you have processed your items, wrap up your work session by clearing away any trash, recycling, and donations from your bathroom. Put away all Other Room items in locations around the house. If you are ready to move on, skip ahead to step 2, Streamline, or put away any items that have an intuitive home and make note of any items that don't. Move any homeless items to a temporary landing zone.

> **PRO TIP:** You can donate your excess, unopened, and non-expired beauty overflow and grooming tools to local shelters and charities in need of these items. Take a deep breath and enjoy the cleared energy of your decluttered bathroom.

Common Bathroom Categories

- Beauty
  - Body
  - Eyes
  - Face
  - Hair
  - Hand and Nail
  - Sun
- Bath Soaps and Salts
- Bath Toys
- Books
- Dental
- First Aid
- Grooming
- Jewelry
- Linens
- Magazines
- Medicine/Prescriptions
- Samples
- Travel

15 THINGS TO LET GO OF NOW

1. Expired or toxic products
2. Expired medicines and prescriptions
3. Products you'll try "someday"
4. Products you tried and don't like
5. Bath gifts you wish you never received
6. Old or broken beauty appliances
7. Stained and ripped towels
8. Moldy shower curtain
9. Old and smelly loofahs
10. Used candles
11. Excess packaging
12. Sample surplus
13. Single-use disposable products (plastic razors I am done with you)
14. Toxic and expired cleaning supplies
15. Self-doubt

Add fun-colored paper for extra joy and inspiration to keep the drawer tidy.

STREAMLINE: OPTIMIZE SPACE IN YOUR BATHROOM

Once you've decluttered your bathroom by removing anything that does not support your goals for the space, it's time to think about optimal storage solutions. It may be necessary to first take inventory of your beauty products. Then you'll be ready to think about zones and storage. If you've used temporary solutions to store items neatly in your space, now is the time to bring in permanent solutions to maximize space.

▷ **START HERE**

1. Complete worksheet 2 (on page 140)
Use your worksheet to guide you through this process to refine your bathroom ecosystem. Identify what has and has not been working. Now that you have decluttered and identified your categories, think about what can be improved by optimizing storage.

2. Create zones
Make a list of all the categories you've identified. Place the Post-it notes in areas of the bathroom where it would make sense to zone your items. Assign zones to each category based on where you're most likely to use them.

3. Maximize space
Repurpose shoe boxes, baskets, and baggies for now. Take notes on any products, storage solutions, or furniture you'll need to maximize your space. Make a list of the optimal storage options for your bathroom, measure as needed, and keep your notes in your notebook.

4. Implement storage solutions
Purchase and install storage solutions. You'll need a home for each category and the right storage solution will make all the difference. I don't know why bathrooms aren't designed with corner caddies, but thank goodness I can buy them. That over-the-toilet shelving didn't come with the house. Think about what solutions you need and there's likely a simple product waiting for you.

> **PRO TIP:** Keep only what you are using now. Remove the overflow and store bulk and backup items in the garage or storage closet to optimize valuable and often limited real estate.

The best way to keep your bath and beauty drawers organized is by adding drawer organizers.

Use paint pens on acrylic organizers to keep your beauty supplies organized and tidy.

5. Label

Adding labels in the bathroom can be helpful, especially because of the volume of items we tend to store here. From sunscreen to hair products, there's no better way to keep things organized than with labels.

Write the date of purchase on the underside of your product with a Sharpie so you'll know when to chuck it.

Use divided storage cabinets with labels for a more efficient morning.

STYLE: CURATE YOUR CALMING BATHROOM

An often overlooked and neglected space, the bathroom can be transformed with minimal effort, and I believe it has the potential to be one of the most nurturing and restorative spaces in your home. With a little help, you can turn your bathroom from a cringe-worthy space into a calming zone of rejuvenation.

▷ **START HERE**

1. Complete worksheet 3 (on page 141)

If a simply styled bathroom sounds appealing, answer the questions in the worksheet. Think about the small steps you can take toward creating a spa-like sanctuary or simply adding a few touches to make it personal. Embrace a few of my tips below or curate your own space with any of the style tips in this book.

2. Replace your towels and soaps

Add new lush towels to instantly brighten and refresh your space. Simple, plush white towels are an easy option, or you can opt for a fun pattern if your bathroom needs pizzazz. Placing a luxury soap in a ceramic dish can turn the average bathroom into a spa oasis.

3. Add candles and plants

Purchase a few of your favorite candles and plants to style and bring serenity into your bathroom. Like I say, "Change the vibe, and your plants will thrive."

> **PRO TIP:** If your thumb isn't green and you are a busy bee, opt for plants that are low-care and soil-free that get most of their water from the air, or succulents that need little maintenance.

4. Streamline your products

Choose one product line or brand of grooming supplies that you love. Think about how hotels keep it clean by only using one product line that satisfies all bathing needs.

> **PRO TIP:** Decant products like bath salts and grooming supplies into matching jars or containers.

5. Swap out your shower curtain and mat

This tiny change can give your space an instant facelift. Choose colors that either energize or calm you, but most importantly, pick something that makes *you* happy.

6. Style with natural materials

Bring the outside in for an extra dose of calm and serenity. I like wood, marble, bamboo, and stone elements in the form of shelving, baskets, and storage.

> **PRO TIP:** Switch to natural pumice stones, real sea sponges, and natural soaps for a back-to-nature experience.

CHAPTER 5

LIVING SPACES

"Having people over reveals the core difference between me and my husband," my friend Jen told me after hosting a dinner party. She focuses on tidying up the house—putting away the kids' toys and frantically vacuuming all the stray crumbs, errant string cheese pieces, and tiny wrappers—all to make her house feel like a home. "This makes me feel ready, excited, and confident to be a hostess," Jen says.

Meanwhile, her husband is busy cooking in the kitchen because he's more concerned about welcoming people into his home with love by sharing his delicious Indian dishes with them. "And the fact that every dish we own is on the counter, looking like a warzone or culinary robbery, is evidence of how much effort (aka love) went into his meal. For me, my demonstration of love is a clean, cozy place for my guests to relax, drink wine, listen to good music, and laugh with friends," she explains.

If you're anything like my friend Jen, the living room is where it's at for you. Another critical energy center of the home, its name says it all: *living* rooms are where we LIVE. How are you living? You're likely familiar with the clutter that accumulates in communal spaces like the living room or entry. A landing spot for life, they are warm and fun, but they can quickly get out of control. With intention and some Simply

Spaced techniques, you and your family can take back control.

TOP CLUTTER CULPRITS

Always on the frontlines, the living room and entry are right up there with the kitchen as heavy traffic zones. From shoes and keys to backpacks and take-out cartons, these living spaces are where the family congregates and the stuff of everyday living lands. Setting up systems to control the chaos will help get the family on-board for shared living. I've identified the top clutter culprits plus a few key tips so that you can thrive in these spaces, get creative, and live the life you want.

Command center chaos

The minutia of life—mail, magazines, pens, receipts—serve a purpose, but never seem to have a home. This landing zone may be your entryway, the coffee or dining table, or couch. No matter what setup you're working with, an organized landing spot can be a game-changer for a busy household.

> **PRO TIP:** Set up a command center for all the things that come in and out on a regular basis: keys, backpacks, shoes, hats, and gloves, the dog leash, etc. These stations are a great example of breaking the rule of grouping like-with-like because in this case, it's better to store certain items right where they are used.

Everything but the kitchen sink

Living spaces are where you gather. They are the hub and entry point for entertaining. They also become a dumping ground for everything that has no home. But your living room isn't the place to store the lawnmower just because it's closest to the front door.

> **PRO TIP:** Keep a selection of toys accessible if this space doubles as a play area. Labeled baskets and bins stored in a tower make cleanup quicker.

Food fallout

I bet there's some form of food product in your couch right now. If you move your sofa, chances are you will you find a bowl's worth of popcorn. Or is that just me? Okay, maybe you are tidier than most, but I'm willing to bet if you look under your cushions or on the floor, you'll see at least one wrapper or a lone jelly bean or chip. If you have kids, make that twenty jelly beans. This is perfectly normal because living areas, TV rooms, and communal spaces tend to be the family gathering spot, so food messes and spills are bound to happen.

> **PRO TIP:** Keep a handheld vacuum in this space. It's a game-changer for an instant tidy or crumb catastrophe.

Dining rooms are designed for connection. Removing distractions and clutter from this space increases the quality of the time spent here.

The traveling campsite

We all know what I'm talking about when I say "traveling campsite" by now. I found one in the bedroom, and now there's another one in the living room. It's comprised of books and bags, cords and iPads, clothes and everything in between. The traveling campsite is a common hang-up in many living spaces.

PRO TIP: Keep a catch-all basket in the entry so you can collect items from around the space and easily make one trip around the house to put things away. Parents: Throw one in the hall to quickly gather up stray toys. Get family buy-in and hold them accountable to the task.

Toys and tots

Kid clutter is real, and it's everywhere. Even if you have the best systems in place, toys, small plastic pieces, and gadgets don't put themselves away. On the other hand, having a home for everything does make cleanup easier and helps to reduce overwhelm. Children need to be able to spread out, play, and create, but they don't need every toy and paint brush at the same time. Refer to Chapter 6 on page 68 for more inspiration on organizing kids' spaces.

PRO TIP: Rather than adding landing spots for toys to pile up, remove bulky entry shelves or replace with a hidden storage bench or ottoman.

GET MOTIVATED!

Think about how you want your home to feel when you first enter it. What does your home say about you and your family? Is it warm and inviting, but a little messy? How do you want it to be? There is no right answer, no right way to live; there's only what's right for you and your unique family. This is an opportunity to think about how you want to feel in and about your space, not a mandate or a comparison game. Tackle this chapter with love and move some of that stuck energy out so that you can be here with a full and present heart.

SIMPLIFY: DECLUTTER YOUR UNLIVABLE LIVING SPACES

It's important to keep in mind that life is meant to be lived. Your house is meant to be lived in. That process doesn't happen without creating a mess, but if you are following the steps in this book, you're already learning a process for tackling clutter. If an organized living room and entry is your goal, let's begin.

▷ **START HERE**

1. Complete worksheet 1 (on page 142)

Before starting each step in this process, identify the goals you have for your living space. Think about why you want to get this space organized and what it will feel like when you do. Complete the worksheet questions for an exercise on defining your "why" and to motivate and inform your decisions. Focus on the joy of family, communal living, and your intentions for this space.

2. Set up your workspace

Use your standard tool kit as referenced on pages 9–10. Label your bins: Donate, Trash, Recycle, Other Room and any additional categories that you'd like to consider. If paper overflow is a common issue here, refer to Chapter 9 on page 94 for tips on how to process and set up a mail station in your entryway. For now, consider adding a shredding pile.

3. Pull everything out and group like-with-like

Begin in one area in your living space and pull everything out, grouping like-with-like. Use the category list included in this chapter to determine what categories of items you have.

4. Process your items

Donate, discard, or recycle any living room items that no longer serve you and your family. As you move through the space, hold each item and ask yourself honestly "Do I love, need, or use this?" If not, let it go. You can include your family in this process or set aside things you need to ask them about.

5. Wrap up

Always allow at least one hour for this step. Once you have processed your items, wrap up your work session by clearing away any trash, recycling, and donations from your living room. Put away all "Other Room" items in homes around the house. If you are ready to move on, skip ahead to step 2, Streamline. Or put away any items that have an intuitive home and take notes in your notebook about any items that don't. Move any homeless items to a temporary landing zone. Take a deep breath and enjoy the cleared energy of your decluttered living space.

When you pull everything out, you are much less likely to put back anything you do not love, need, or use.

COMMON LIVING ROOM CATEGORIES

- Art Supplies
- Backpacks
- Batteries
- Books
- Clothes
- Decor
- Entertainment
- Games
- Keys
- Lightbulbs
- Mail
  - Incoming
  - Outgoing
  - Packages
  - Magazines
- Music
- Office Supplies
- Paper
- Pet Accessories
- Tools
- Toys

Maximize space in a narrow wall by adding shelving or a desk with built-in storage.

15 THINGS TO LET GO OF NOW

1. Toys and games kids have outgrown
2. Old pet toys
3. Dried-out art and office supplies
4. Decor that doesn't match your style
5. Books you'll never read
6. Magazines and newspapers you'll never read
7. Cords and cables from old devices
8. Old or broken electronics
9. Movies you no longer watch
10. Music you no longer listen to
11. Expired coupons, old receipts, menus, and manuals
12. Unidentifiable keys
13. Plastic party favors
14. Dead plants
15. Comparison

STREAMLINE: OPTIMIZE SPACE IN YOUR LIVING AREAS

The living room is likely the last space you walk through before leaving your house and the first room you enter once you get home. How should this space feel? Does it welcome you home at the end of a busy day? Does it feel warm and cozy or uninviting and frazzled?

It's time to start thinking about the ways in which you can maximize space to accommodate the activities and intentions you have for them. There are many ways to use empty wall space in these common areas, so look around and imagine how you want this space to operate so that it supports your life.

▷ **START HERE**

1. Complete worksheet 2 (on page 143)
Use your worksheet to guide you through this process to refine your living room ecosystem. Identify what has and has not been working. Now that you have decluttered and identified your categories, think about what can be improved by optimizing storage.

2. Create zones
You've already established what items you'd like to keep in this space, but maybe you don't have the right storage yet. Identify the areas you'd like to create with your Post-its. Perhaps you want to create a mail-processing center? Or a backpack landing spot? Keep track of the list in your notebook. You can break the rule of "group like-with-like" if it makes sense to keep certain items accessible. For example, maybe you only need one leash by the front door and can keep your other pet supplies in the pantry or garage.

> **PRO TIP:** If you have a dog and it makes sense to keep your leashes and walking supplies close by the door, create a functional entryway setup.

3. Maximize space
If you have an empty wall by the front door, you may be able to add a small desk or wall unit. If you have more toys than storage, add bins to your list. If a command center sounds like a good addition to this space, there are many components to consider.

Living spaces do well with hidden storage like bins, desks, and storage furniture. Think ottomans and coffee tables that open to more storage or shelves with cubbies. Baskets go a long way in spaces like this for quick pick up. Take measurements of any

wall space, drawers, shelves, or desks that will require additional products.

> **PRO TIP:** Visit www.simplyspaced.com/shop for some of my favorite ways to optimize this kind of space.

I love this entry we helped design for a client. There is so much you can do to maximize a small space. Slat walls, hooks, and labeled baskets transform this nook.

Associate an activity with each area in your space.

4. Implement storage solutions

Set aside at least an hour or two to make sure all the options you've bought work and support the space. This process will most likely take place over the course of a few days. Most places take returns, so don't worry if you don't nail every solution on the first try.

5. Label

One way to get the family on the same page, especially kids, is to use labels to identify exactly where things should go. We often think an organizational system that is obvious to us should be to others as well, but that's not always the case. Over time, people forget which storage containers in the house are designated to hold which items, and before you know it, the hat bin is filled with broken crayons and markers. Labels remind us there is a home for everything.

> **PRO TIP:** Let your kids watch you make and apply labels; it's a great way to get them to start thinking, learning, and developing habits around organization.

STYLE: CURATE YOUR LIVING SPACES

If this is a space where you gather with friends or family, it's a great place to highlight those special items that celebrate your life and the people in it. Remember, the task is to identify and highlight three special or meaningful items that are in alignment with your goals for each space, and a selection of your life. Maybe it is a painting, a photograph, or gallery wall dedicated to your child's art. Using items like these is a great way to think about how to start styling your space. Based on the many spaces I've organized, I've rounded up my best style tips for making your living room feel peaceful, happy, and balanced. Keep a list of all your ideas in your notebook. Styling takes time; it's not a one-and-done undertaking, so take notes to capture all your inspiration.

▷ **START HERE**

1. Complete worksheet 3 (on page 144)
Fill out the worksheets to kickstart your living room styling. Think about what elements will make this space feel like a home and what you can feature to make it your own.

2. Frame your favorite family and friend photos
If you intend for this space to be a place where loved ones convene, bring in some photos or art to reflect this intention. A gallery wall or oversized, beautifully framed photo may just do the trick.

The home is a mirror of self and the books on our shelves help tell our story. What story does your home tell?

3. Make your pillows talk

One of the best and quickest ways to jazz up and transform any living space is by adding in beautiful pillows or a pretty throw. If you don't have a clear vision for your personal style, experiment with pillow patterns and textures to see what sticks.

4. Add plants

Adding a plant or two to this space will bring life to the room. Not only do they increase air quality, they also help lower risk for illnesses and improve people's moods.

> **PRO TIP:** Choose easy-to-care-for plants for the living room, like snake plants, Philodendron, and Majesty Palm.

5. Choose new lighting

A new light fixture can help brighten the space and create a warm, welcoming vibe. Hang a chandelier or add a lamp, or two, to transform and personalize your space.

6. Choose a neutral color palette

Color is a powerful tool for transforming any space, but too many colors can easily overwhelm it. Stick to a limited color palette for walls, couches, and flooring to give your room a cohesive look. Add personality with pops of color from art, photos, and accessories.

Go from dinner to dining by adding flowers and candles.

Pillows and plants bring life, color, and texture to any space.

CHAPTER 6

KIDS' SPACES

Kids' spaces are notorious mess magnets. Let's face it, our kids are the messiest ones in the house, yet we can learn so much design-wise from their creative minds and freedom to color outside of the lines. Whenever I work with kids, I am always surprised at how willing they are to get involved, learn, donate, and share with other children. They crave order and want others to respect their belongings just as much as adults do. And just like us they won't magically create systems without guidance. Teaching them a few tips just might help you cohabitate with a bit more grace.

I'll never forget New Year's Eve two years ago when my family sat around the living room contemplating what we should do that night. Everyone went around the room and offered an idea. As a joke, I said, "Let's organize Barbies." When it came time to vote on what we would be doing, my suggestion won. I'm not saying organizing dolls should be everyone's pastime, but at the end of a long year, I think my family needed a good purge to get rid of the old and make room for the new.

That same night, when my niece put one of her favorite old toys in the donation bin and I reminded her that she didn't have to give it away, she said "It's okay. I want other kids to experience joy." Her generosity and gratitude floored me.

Naturally curious, children can quickly learn new things—maybe even better than adults. This makes me wonder why we need to feel so in control. I understand that someone needs to be in charge because we can't live in chaos, and the kids aren't responsible for paying the bills or making dinner. But they teach us to accept that life is messy, so we should stop trying for perfection.

As a parent, you can teach your children systems of thinking even if you are still learning them yourself. There are simple tricks we can employ to help maintain household sanity, and teachable methods that can benefit your children now and throughout their lives.

TOP CLUTTER CULPRITS

From the time they come out of the womb to the time they leave the house, kids are constantly growing—in and out of clothes, toys, gadgets, and trends. They change fast, and they're magnets for clutter. For adults who change relatively little in comparison, trying to contain all of their stuff feels like you're pushing a boulder up a hill. And just when you think you've made it to the top, it's Christmas again! Here are five clutter culprits along with five tips to tame the kid mess now:

Clothing chaos
Kids grow quickly, and their ever-changing wardrobe can be a pain point for parents. Not always ready for how quickly kids grow out of clothes, parents often over-buy and get a massive

influx of clothing from generous friends and family that's hard to part with. Maybe you'll have another baby and need that duck-billed onesie one day or maybe you won't. Either way, the pile of clothes grows quickly, and the key is to keep it under control.

PRO TIP: Set limits. One way to prevent clothing overwhelm is to decide ahead of time how much clothing you want to hang on to beyond what you currently use. I like to designate one bin for the major age changes (18 months, 24 months, 36 months, etc.) in case my client has a second (or third) child.

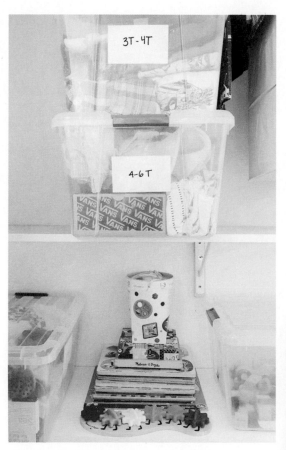

Designate bins and keep only what you will love, need, and use.

The joy of toys
Most parents want to give their kids everything. It's a generous and benevolent idea. You are making up for what you didn't have as a child, and you work hard to provide them with the best. Although this mentality comes from a place of love, the reality is, most kids in our overstimulated world need less stuff and more structure. Never-ending access to toys can set kids up for unrealistic expectations throughout their lives. It's really that simple.

PRO TIP: Try implementing toy rotations (one in and one out) and set limits on how many new toys come in. Edit the toy room or game room often and encourage children to appreciate the joy of donating to children in need.

System breakdown
One thing that's extremely helpful when it comes to organizing for kids is accessible systems. It's empowering when kids can access their things and put them away when they are old enough. I often see parents create elaborate systems for organizing, but they forget to think about what will work best for the children or include them in the process.

PRO TIP: When you are organizing any kids' space, think about how you can design it so that they can learn to maintain it.

You did not grow up in the same world your children live in. Home life today is filled with an unprecedented level of distractions. If you struggle with focus and attention, imagine what it's like to be a child with endless access to information, television, technology, video games, and toys. Children benefit from simplicity just as much as adults do. I am not talking about depravity, but like us, children need space to learn, grow, play, and imagine. Satisfying a child's every wish and desire with material objects can stifle their imaginations and inhibit their sense of hope, wonder, and creativity. Think about ways to set limits and take back control of the inundation.

LEGO mania

The question I get asked all the time is, "How do I organize my kid's LEGOs?" There are a million different ways to keep them organized, but first you need storage that can accommodate them.

> **PRO TIP:** Use a LEGO board or designate a shelf to display one or two (not all) built creations. Try stacking, rolling bins, or organizing individual sets in small containers.

Book bewilderment

Kids these days have more books than most adults I know. Although it's great to have lots of reading materials, keeping them organized can be a chore.

> **PRO TIP:** Store kids' books in open magazine files to keep them from flopping around and falling over on the bookshelves.

SIMPLIFY: DECLUTTER YOUR KIDS' CHAOTIC ROOM OR PLAYROOM

By reducing the overflow, setting limits, and designating homes for everything, adults can teach children to appreciate and care for their belongings. Getting your children involved in the process is a great way to encourage responsibility while showing that you respect their opinions. It's up to you to decide how involved you want them to be, but you may be surprised by how much your children appreciate learning how to organize.

▷ **START HERE**

1. Complete worksheet 1 (on page 145)

Before starting each step in this process, identify the goals you have for your kids' room or playroom. Think about why you want to get this space organized and what it will feel like when you do. Complete the worksheet for an exercise in defining your "why" and to motivate and inform your decisions. Get really clear about your intentions for this space.

> **PRO TIP:** Ask your child how he or she would like the space to look. You may be surprised by the answer.

2. Set up your workspace

Use your standard tool kit as referenced on pages 9–10. Label your bins: Donate, Trash, Recycle, Other Room, and any additional categories that you'd like to consider.

> **PRO TIP:** Depending on the age of your children, you might want to take a stab at this step solo or with your accountability partner. Involving young children this early on can be unsettling and distracting. But if your kids are old enough, an organizing session is a fun mental and physical exercise to do together.

3. Pull everything out and group like-with-like

Begin in one area in your kids' space and pull everything out, grouping like-with-like. Use the category list included in this chapter to determine which categories of items you have. Pulling everything together by category will help you determine how much of each category you have. Through this process, there's a good chance

Begin by pulling everything out and organizing items into groups.

you'll find random items like missing puzzle pieces and heads to decapitated dolls.

> **PRO TIP:** Set aside items that have sentimental value and label them as mementos. Make an assessment when you get to Chapter 11, Mementos, on page 114.

4. Process your items

Donate, discard, or recycle any kids' items that your children no longer love, need, or use. As you move through the space, think about the items that no longer fit, inspire, or serve your child or your family. Keep only what your children love and play with now. Once you have done a solo, parental decluttering pass, take some time to work with your child or children to sort through any questionable items like toys, clothes, and games to determine if they should stay or go.

> **PRO TIP:** Teaching kids to help other people is invaluable and you'll be amazed how motivated they may be.

5. Wrap up

Always allow at least one hour for this step. Once you have processed your items, wrap up your work session by clearing away any trash, recycling, and donations from your kids' space. Put away all "Other Room" items in locations around the house. If you are ready to move on, skip ahead to step 2, Streamline, or put away any items that have an intuitive home and take notes in your notebook about any items that don't. Move any homeless items to a temporary landing zone.

> **PRO TIP:** Add your own musical flare to this song my friends Jen and Dodo sing with their daughter, Maya: "Clean up. Clean up. Everybody, clean up." Repeat. Take a deep breath and enjoy the cleared energy of your decluttered kids' space.

15 THINGS TO LET GO OF NOW:

1. Broken or defective toys
2. Toys and learning games your kids have aged out of
3. Toys, technology, and puzzles with missing pieces
4. Duplicate toys
5. Dolls without heads and limbs
6. Outgrown clothing and shoes
7. Outdated technology
8. Dried-out markers, paint, and playdough
9. The duck-billed onesie (okay fine, keep it)
10. Party favor bags
11. Piles of kids' art (use your memento boxes to save the best)
12. Gifts from your in-laws no one likes
13. Activity books and projects you'll never do (stop feeling guilty, no one wants to do them)
14. At least half of the toys
15. Perfectionism

COMMON KID CATEGORIES:

- Accessories
  - Bows
  - Bracelets
  - Hats
  - Sunglasses
  - Watches
- Arts and Crafts
  - Activity Books
  - Artwork
  - Coloring Books
  - Crayons
  - Markers
  - Paint
  - Paper
  - Pencils
  - Pens
  - Stickers
- Books
- Clothes*
- Dress Up
- Gadgets
- Games
- Grooming
- Learning Tools
- Mementos*
- Music
- Puzzles
- Toys
  - Balls
  - Cars
  - Dinosaurs
  - Dolls
  - Figurines
  - Kitchen
  - LEGOs
  - Stuffed Animals
  - Superheroes
  - Tools
  - Trains
- Playdough

Refer to corresponding chapter

Enlist your accountability partner to help you organize.

STREAMLINE: OPTIMIZE SPACE IN YOUR KIDS' ROOM OR PLAYROOM

When it comes to kids' spaces, I think a lot about functional storage. Because children grow so quickly, modular shelving, dual-function storage, and labeled bins and baskets are fundamental building blocks for sustainable live and play spaces. Keeping toys accessible to little ones and designating a home for everything, not only gives kids an opportunity to understand and learn organizational principles, it also encourages them to be responsible for maintaining them.

Durable bins are perfect storage solutions for kids' spaces.

▷ **START HERE**

1. Complete worksheet 2 (on page 146)
Use your worksheet to guide you through this process to refine your kiddy ecosystem. Identify what has and has not been working. Now that you have decluttered and identified your categories, think about what you can improve by optimizing storage.

2. Create zones
Children respond well to simple systems. Think about the categories of items you have in any given kids' space and the types of items you'd like your kids to have access to. Then, use Post-its to identify the categories you want to control, like messy paints, playdough, and water guns. You can also determine the categories you want your kids to be able to reach easily like dinosaurs, costumes, and books. Map out zones in the room based on the items you've sorted through and categorized. You can break the rule of "group like-with-like" for kids when you want to keep

their most frequently used toys and clothes front and center. It's also not a bad idea to keep certain items down low or on display for easy access.

3. Maximize space
Once you've identified the zones you want to create in the space, write down any product ideas or solutions that you will need. Kids' spaces are ideal for small shelving units, rolling carts, adjustable shelving—essentially anything sturdy enough to contain and categorize all the tiny bits. Think floor-level storage, easy access bins with labels, durable bins, and baskets small enough for little hands. Take inventory of all the types of items in your space and measure any wall space, drawers, shelves, or desks that will require additional products to keep things neat and livable.

Low shelving allows kids to find their favorite toys.

4. Implement storage solutions

Set aside at least an hour or two to make sure all the options you've bought work and support the space.

5. Label

Children love to know where to find their most prized possessions, and if you give these items a home, kids are more likely to maintain the systems you've created. Labels are especially helpful for other family members, guests, the housekeeper, or a babysitter.

Reserve higher shelving for storing lesser-used items.

Name each group of items with a word that will remind you of its contents and provide a landing spot and permanent home for the item.

STYLE: CURATE YOUR KIDS' ROOM OR PLAYROOM

I love to organize kids' spaces to see what inspires, motivates, and ignites their imaginations. Some kids love to collect treasures, and some love photos and stickers. Some kids love to keep mementos, while others are budding minimalists. It's important to understand and respect each child's own unique story, needs, and capacity, while holding him or her accountable for maintaining and honoring their possessions.

One way to encourage pride in ownership is to ask your child to identify the three most important items in his or her space. Finding a special home or display for these items shows that you respect them and teaches children a key organizational principle: a home for everything and everything in its place. Here are my best style tips for kids' spaces.

▷ **START HERE**

1. Complete worksheet 3 (on page 147)
If you are struggling to find inspiration for styling your kids' spaces, complete the worksheet at the end of this book and start with your why. Follow my tips below and get your kids involved.

2. Create a kid-friendly gallery wall
A gallery wall doesn't have to be daunting. Tape up your kids' favorite art next to yours. Frame your favorite family photos or hang a special memento from your own childhood.

3. Put puzzles on display
Get a rack or stand for wooden puzzles. This will create beautiful shelf decor and a neat home for puzzle pieces that may otherwise get lost.

A can of chalkboard paint can totally transform a kids' space into magical and fun learning and drawing tool.

KIDS' SPACES

4. Unbox your games

To make room in a small space, get rid of the extra packaging for small games and sets and opt to store them in cohesive bins or baskets.

5. Display wooden toys

Ditch the plastic and display well-made, durable wooden toys on shelves and surfaces. They look prettier, last longer, and are more eco-friendly than their plastic counterparts.

6. Embrace the rainbow

You don't have to go crazy with a rainbow palette, but subtle, colorful details go a long way in adding life to any play space. Bring in color-coded books, a rainbow garland, or a decal for the wall.

Designate an empty wall as a learning center by adding shelves, craft storage, or a mini-library.

CHAPTER 7

STORAGE AND UTILITY SPACES

I asked my Instagram followers to fill in the following blank: "If my house is my castle, my garage is my_____." The most amazing answers included: "moat," "trash heap," "dragon's lair," and "husband's." I'm sharing a photo of yours truly in my own garage on the next page. Do you see that joy on my face? That's the happiness that comes from finally getting on top of your storage space and saying goodbye to all the extras that crowd out the important items we need to thrive in our lives. The struggle is real. I know, I lived it. Prior to this photo, I spent years frustrated by the state of my garage.

Although storage spaces are the most neglected areas of our homes, there's no reason to believe you can't get yours in order if it's a priority for you. An organized garage, utility closet, or storage unit can be a game-changer, especially if you are short on space elsewhere in your home.

As a professional organizer who hauls away clutter for a living, I use my garage as a temporary dumping ground for e-waste, hazardous waste, returns, kit supplies—you name it, I've got it. And without systems in place, I would go out of my mind. Once I got my garage set up and organized, it became much easier to get back to baseline with a quick tidying up. I hope my tips will inspire you to think outside of the box and make your garage, storage spaces, and utility closets work for—not against—you.

TOP CLUTTER CULPRITS

Most families have at least one area—a closet, hallway, utility shelf, garage, crawlspace, shed, or basement—that's packed with stuff. There isn't much I haven't seen in my profession, but I've found that clearing out a client's storage space comes with its own set of unique surprises. But I can guarantee that diving head-first into these spaces and getting your hands dirty pays off, especially if you want to shift your home's energy. When you tackle storage spaces and clear them out, you release stagnant energy and free up your own physical and mental space.

The dumping ground

It happens slowly, but surely. What was once a home for your grandmother's china, is now a sea of taped-up boxes and bins where you couldn't find that china if you tried. Being willing to let go is a critical part of the process.

> **PRO TIP:** Beware of shifted items, heavy boxes, bugs, rodents, toxic chemicals, and forgotten items from the past. If you are up for the challenge, tackle this space just like you would any other, but remember to wear gloves (or a gasmask in some cases).

Toxic takeover

From paints and cleaners to bug sprays and detergents, storage spaces are magnets for toxins and hazardous materials. Don't worry about the more egregious piles of stuff for now and get rid of these items first for the safety and health of your family.

PRO TIP: Find a local safe recycling center that will take your hazardous waste.

The someday, maybe fallacy

I've seen it time and time again. People hold on to items that they may use someday, but never actually do. It gets put in a storage space somewhere in the house, only to be forgotten. I encourage you to find those items and put them out where they can be used or decide to let them go.

PRO TIP: Be honest with yourself about what you really need. Be okay with having to buy another pair of garden aeration slippers in six years when you think you'll use them . . . you won't.

Poor space planning

Nowhere in the house is there a greater opportunity for maximizing and optimizing space than in a garage, storage, or utility space. Use of vertical and horizontal space is paramount.

PRO TIP: Look up when planning these multi-use spaces; think overhead and above doors, along walls, and inside cabinets. Every inch is precious here, but it does require a little planning.

Clutter creep

It happens slowly—year after year—one carton of Holiday cheer at time. One day you're moving into a house with a spacious two-car garage, and the next you can't walk through it. How did you ever live without a singing Santa, anyway?

PRO TIP: Set up a TaskRabbit, schedule a pick-up, or ask a helpful friend to drop donations off for you. This initial purge might be the motivation you need to kick decluttering into gear.

SIMPLIFY: DECLUTTER YOUR UNSIGHTLY STORAGE SPACE

If you are about to tackle your storage space, garage, or utility closet, make sure you do it with the right intentions. Freeing up space in these areas may be hard at first, but it's a game-changer. Commit to your intentions for the space and keep only what you love, need, or use. That's not to say you cannot keep sentimental items or an extra shoe rack, but letting go of anything that has not been used in years may align more with your goals than hanging onto something that can be easily replaced down the line.

The garage is a notorious landing spot for stuck energy, toxic chemicals, and the "someday, maybes." Clear the clutter with intention and keep only what you love, need, and use.

▷ **START HERE**

1. Complete worksheet 1 (on page 148)
Before starting each step in this process, identify the goals you have for your storage area. Think about why you want to get this space organized and what it will feel like when you do. Do you want to fit two cars in your garage? Are you clearing the space to finally set up your emergency kits? Complete the worksheet to get clear about your intentions.

2. Set up your workspace
Use your standard tool kit as referenced on pages 9–10. Label your bins: Donate, Trash, Recycle, Other Room, and any additional categories that you'd like to consider. Sell, Toss, Recycle, and Hazardous Waste are common ones. Other categories that come up a lot are Electronic and Garden Waste.

> **PRO TIP:** Think about wearing gloves, a face mask, and sturdy shoes while doing any project that involves a treacherous storage space.

3. Pull everything out and group like-with-like
Begin in one area in your storage space and pull everything out, grouping like-with-like. Use the category list included in this chapter to determine which categories of items you have.

> **PRO TIP:** Decluttering storage spaces can be a big undertaking, so be prepared for a longer time investment. This is a great space to bring in a friend, family member, or an accountability partner.

4. Process your items
Donate, trash, or recycle any storage item that you do not love, need, or use. As you move through this space, think about items that have been stored for too long that you're most likely never going to use again. If your overall goal is to declutter and clear the space, use that intention as motivation to let things go. Recirculate that energy elsewhere and keep only the things that align with your lifestyle.

5. Wrap up

Always allow at least one hour for this step. Once you have processed your items, wrap up your work session by clearing away any trash, recycling, donations, and hazardous waste from your storage area. Put away all "Other Room" items in locations around the house. If you are ready to move on, skip ahead to step 2, Streamline, or put away any items that have an intuitive home and take notes in your notebook about any items that don't. Move any homeless items to a temporary landing zone.

PRO TIP: If you have a lot of oversized items to let go of or bulk donations, consider setting up a pickup from your local donation center. You can also call 1-800-Got-Junk or hire a Task Rabbit to haul away items. Take a deep breath and enjoy the cleared energy of your decluttered storage space.

15 THINGS TO LET GO OF NOW:

1. Toxic chemicals and hazardous waste*
2. Old electronics and cords
3. Old paint cans (take a picture of any current colors)*
4. Duplicate tools or tools that never get used
5. Bins of clothes that will never be worn
6. Gifts that will never be used
7. Excess camping chairs (how many do you really need?)
8. Old china and silver that you are saving for when the Queen visits
9. Unused exercise equipment
10. Decor that no longer matches your style
11. Anything broken that's not worth repairing
12. Moldy or soiled holiday items
13. Leftover tiles, carpet, and home decor samples
14. Sentimental items that are no longer sentimental (everything else goes into your memento bins)
15. Living in the past

*Dispose of chemicals, hazardous waste, and old paints safely. Find your local SAFE center or local dropoff.

COMMON STORAGE CATEGORIES:

- Auto
- Backup Supplies
- Batteries
- Bikes
- Camping
- Cleaning
- Clothes
- Electronics
- Emergency Supplies
- Exercise
- Gardening
- Hand and Power Tools
- Holiday
- Home Decor
- Kids/Baby Gear
- Lightbulbs
- Mementos
- Paint
- Paper*
- Party Supplies
- Pet Supplies
- Photos
- Seasonal Gear
- Sewing
- Shoes
- Sports Equipment
- Toys
- Travel

*Refer to corresponding chapter

STREAMLINE: OPTIMIZE SPACE IN YOUR STORAGE AREAS

I have seen it all, from full-scale slat walls to under-the-floor crawl space shelving. So — when it comes to streamlining your storage space, it's important to utilize your wall space like nobody's business. The simplest of solutions can transform your space.

Retrofit vertical storage areas with shelving to maximize space. We added labeled, weathertight storage bins to make the most of this tiny closet.

▷ **START HERE**

1. Complete worksheet 2 (on page 149)
Use your worksheet to guide you through this process of redefining your storage ecosystem. Identify what has and has not been working. Now that you have decluttered and identified your categories, think about what you can improve by optimizing storage.

2. Create zones
Before you even think about what product to get, use your Post-its to zone out each category on your list. Put your once-a-year items up high or overhead but keep your emergency food and supplies within reach. Being strategic about where you put items will inspire you to maintain your space.

3. Maximize space
Once you've identified the zones you want to create in the space, write down any product ideas or solutions that you will need. Wire shelves, hooks, pegboards, workbenches, rods, racks, and bins can maximize the space on otherwise useless walls. Measure any wall space, drawers, shelves, or desks that will require additional products and take inventory of the items that don't have a home. A pegboard or hanging wall unit is the perfect way to organize tools and everyday items like brooms, mops, and cleaning supplies. When it comes to storage spaces, it would be a good idea to look into a custom modular system to retrofit your space. Accessibility is the name of the game.

> **PRO TIP:** Think weathertight storage and dust- / water-resistant materials when choosing products for exposed or long-term storage.

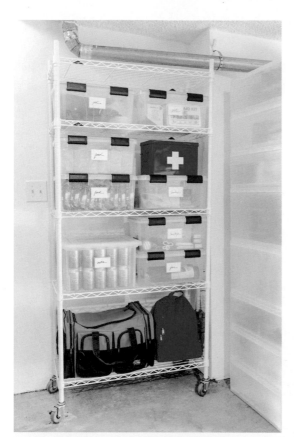

4. Implement storage solutions

Set aside at least an hour or two to make sure all the options you've bought work and support the space. You may want to hire a handyperson to install or assemble shelving.

> **PRO TIP:** I use TaskRabbit to maximize my time and save my energy for big jobs.

5. Label

Labels are fantastic tools for storage spaces. Particularly useful in a space like the garage, a label makes it easy to access and take inventory of items in those hard-to-reach spaces.

Make use of wall space by optimizing space efficiently using shelving, stackable containers, hooks, and wall racks.

I maximized the space in this garage by implementing a wall-to-wall super stylish peg system to hold bikes, helmets, sporting equipment, and more.

STYLE: CURATE YOUR SUSTAINABLE STORAGE SPACE

Most of us aren't thinking about the garage when we think about home decorating, but utilitarian spaces can be beautiful and transform mundane, everyday chores. If you're tired of feeling like Cinderella, upgrade your utility space and start mopping floors like the boss you are. If you feel overwhelmed by a barrage of household chores, you're less likely to maintain it. The good news is, even your most practical spaces can harness the energy of an empowered space with minimal effort.

▷ **START HERE**

1. Complete worksheet 3 (on page 150)
Start by completing the worksheet at the back of this book as an exercise in rethinking your storage and utility centers. Imagine your space the way you'd want it and answer the questions to guide you. Use the ideas below to get your wheels turning.

2. Choose a modern storage system
Gone are the days of old-school garages. It's just as easy to create something awesome and modern yourself as it is to spend $20K on a custom built-in overhaul. Inexpensive, clean modern solutions make it easy and inexpensive to revamp an otherwise dull space with a modular and inexpensive full-wall system.

3. Make a giant pegboard wall
Pegboard walls, even the DIY variety, are very popular at Simply Spaced.

4. Add wallpaper
Wallpaper is one of my favorite hacks to brighten and completely transform a utilitarian space. Add a pop of color as a quick fix for an otherwise boring space, such as a laundry room or linen closet. Nowadays, they come in every color, pattern, and permanence so the options are endless.

5. Tidy your tools
They aren't just for Pinterest, and they don't have be shoved in a box. A tool display can be both functional and aesthetically pleasing with little effort. Hang up the tools you use for a neat, functional display.

> **PRO TIP:** Wood and metal tools as well as cleaning supplies look just as good in a utility closet as they do on a wall in the hallway. Ditch the plastic for a more sustainable option.

6. Style your walls
Uplevel your storage areas by adding oversized art or create gallery walls with the prints that don't make the cut elsewhere. Hang a surfboard or display your collections on empty walls. All those prints and frames in the garage? Put them up or phase them out.

Adopt the "a home for everything" mantra, even for lost socks.

CHAPTER 8

OFFICE

With more people working both full-time and part-time from home, most of us have some sort of office area at home, whether it's an entire room dedicated to work or shared space like my own that doubles as a guest room. No matter how your home is configured, if work must be done, an office area can be created. To get any real work done, it's important to understand that a space of your own is a critical component to productivity. In an overly distracted world where family obligations, social media, texts, and emails constantly vie for our attention, a conducive at-home work zone can be the difference between getting promoted and staying stuck in the chaotic now.

TOP CLUTTER CULPRITS

When it comes to home office clutter, what I see most often is a case of the dumps. When there's no landing spot for mail and packages that pile up, the office becomes the dumping ground. The psychological effects are feelings of overwhelm, fear, anxiety, and avoidance. Getting work done is nearly impossible when there's a mountain of paper to sort through and a mile-long list of to-dos. It's imperative to clear the clutter to honor the work you intend to do. To kickstart your awareness of what's holding you back, here are five common clutter culprits, plus five tips you can employ immediately to get back to work:

Desk disarray

I have heard people say that they are more creative with a cluttered desk. Trust me, I wish this was true for me. Let's just assume that if you picked up this book, you're the type of person who sees every pen, pop-up ad, and picture as a potential derailment. I'm talking to the person who will take twenty minutes to get back to work after getting a notification on the iPad that a celebrity liked her Instagram photo, to come to realize it was just her mom who had a question about her lasagna recipe. Remember, tidy desk, tidy mind.

> **PRO TIP:** Every time you sit down for a work session, clear all potential distractions from your view, including paperwork, phones, and other devices.

A neatly organized space can inspire productivity and action.

GET MOTIVATED!

Work toward your big goals like a boss. Even if your home isn't perfect, all you need to get started is a clear corner somewhere. Don't let your cluttered house be a reason to put off your dreams. Take tiny steps each day in the direction you are headed. If clutter has got you down, a good old-fashioned purge may be just what you need to remember how capable you are.

The multi-use space

If you are like me, you probably yearn for a space in your house that's 100 percent your own. For city dwellers and larger families, this may seem like a pipe dream. But if passion and purpose is what you're after, a room of your own (or even a desk) is imperative to realizing your dreams. You want to make the magic happen? Make your home happen for you.

PRO TIP: Dedicate one area in your home specifically to work that will advance your career. We've turned closets into high-functioning offices and converted dining rooms into divided workspaces. Think outside the box.

The cord conundrum

Is there anything more chaotic than a cord web? All I can think of is the meme of tangled cords that says, "This is my mind on clutter."

PRO TIP: Wrangle your cords and use binder clips, zip ties, cord organizers, and cord boxes to tame the cord chaos. If you don't know about The Fuse Reel Sidewinder, you're welcome.

Digital distractions

Unproductivity at home can stem from visible clutter, but then add in digital distractions and it's a miracle anything gets done.

PRO TIP: If you are trying to work through a challenge in this book, cut out the distractions by switching your phone to airplane mode and going offline.

Poor planning and productivity

One of the reasons we feel like we never get anything done is our never-ending to-do list. Task-based lists are great, but if everything is important, nothing really is.

PRO TIP: Schedule what matters. Add a time block to your calendar for important to-dos and uphold them like you would an appointment.

SIMPLIFY: DECLUTTER YOUR OUT-OF-CONTROL OFFICE

If your eye is on a dream that's bigger than yourself, you need a commitment that's bigger than your stuff. Clearing a space to create your best work means letting go of anything that stands in your way. Ask yourself what you want to show up for you that you don't currently see. What do you see around you that's in conflict with that dream? Everything in your work area should support the life you want to lead. Broken pens and piles of clutter have an energetic resonance that's misaligned with the realization of your dreams.

▷ **START HERE**

1. Complete worksheet 1 (on page 151)
Before starting each step in this process, identify the goals you have for your office. Think about why you want to get this space organized and what it will feel like when you do. Complete the worksheet questions for an exercise in defining your "why" and to motivate and inform your decisions. Focus on your optimal working environment and what will be most conducive to your creativity and productivity.

2. Set up your workspace
Use your standard tool kit as referenced on pages 9–10. Label your bins: Donate, Trash, Recycle, Other Room, and any additional categories that you'd like to consider.

PRO TIP: Save any items you've collected that inspire you or represent your personal or career goals. Consider creating a vision board that will guide you toward realizing your dreams.

3. Pull everything out and group like-with-like
Begin in one area in your office and pull everything out, grouping like-with-like. You can start with a cabinet, drawer, or the entire space. Use the category list included in this chapter to determine what categories of items you have.

PRO TIP: Set a separate date with yourself to sort paper. If you can make a quick decision about something, deal with it now and set aside the stacks and piles that require more attention for a dedicated paper session.

5. Wrap up
Always allow at least one hour for this step. Once you have processed your items, wrap up your work session by clearing away any trash, recycling, and donations. Put away all "Other Room" items in locations around the house. If you are ready to move on, skip ahead to step 2, Streamline, or put away any items that have an intuitive home and take notes in your notebook about items that don't. Move any homeless items to a temporary landing zone.

4. Process your items
Donate, discard, or recycle any office items that you do not love, need, or use. As you work through this space, remember what you've determined was important for your future aspirations. Anything that is not in alignment with that goal should not live in this space. Take notes in your notebook of anything you'll need to buy or replace.

PRO TIP: This is a great time to burn some sage or Palo Santo to clear the energy and release old intentions, stale dreams, and unproductive, self-sabotaging habits. Take a deep breath and enjoy the cleared energy of your decluttered office.

COMMON OFFICE CATEGORIES:

- Books
- Business Cards
- Cleaning Supplies
- Computer Accessories
- Cords
- Decor
- Electronics
- Entertainment (music/movies)
- Files
- Inspirational Items
- Magazines/Newspapers
- Mementos
- Office Supplies
- Paperwork*
- Photos
- Stationery
- To Do

*Refer to corresponding chapter

15 THINGS TO LET GO OF NOW

1. Books that don't align with work and career goals
2. Uninspiring art
3. Broken, used-up pens and pencils
4. Empty ink cartridges
5. Old calendars
6. Used notebooks
7. Shredding that needs to get shredded
8. Antiquated technology
9. Old software
10. Meaningless tchotchkes
11. Broken tools or equipment
12. Excess paper and supplies
13. Cords and cables that have no use
14. Dead or fake plants
15. Fear of change

Make the most of any wall or closet space by adding modular shelving. This closet was just a hanging rod before shelving turned it into a multi-functional live/work space that utilized form and function in every inch.

STREAMLINE: OPTIMIZE SPACE IN YOUR OFFICE

With the excess and overflow out of the way, you are now ready to set up your office for productive, creative work. The next step in organizing is to optimize this space by creating homes and accessible systems to keep you motivated and on track.

▷ **START HERE**

1. Complete worksheet 2 (on page 152)
Use your worksheet to guide you through this process to refine your office ecosystem. Identify what has and has not been working. Now that you have decluttered and identified your categories, think about what can be improved by optimizing storage.

2. Create zones
Make a list of all the categories you've identified in your office space and create a Post-it note for each one. Use your sticky notes to identify the most optimal zones for each category. Start with the most important—your desk or work table. Find an area with indirect light, ample storage, and a comfortable chair.

> **PRO TIP:** Maximize vertical space on an empty wall, inside a closet, or on a bookshelf.

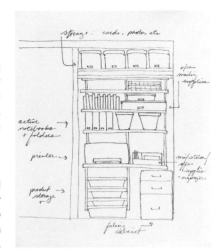

3. Maximize space
Start by moving shelves and identify areas where you could use a shelf riser or other space-saving functionality. Write down all the supplies you'll need to store, see, or access everything in each zone in your notebook. Measure your space and take a photographic inventory of your office on your phone. Even though I recommend keeping your desk free of clutter, it's also important to keep a few select items within arm's reach, like a notebook, your favorite pen, a candle, or item of inspiration. If you have an active filing system, get a desktop processing station. And if you're going to process mail here, too, consider getting one with grab-and-go supplies.

> **PRO TIP:** Burning a scented candle while you work helps keep you motivated. I often light a candle as a ritual to signify the start of my work session. Associating hard work with a positive smell or experience can result in a desired outcome.

4. Implement storage solutions
Once you have your storage solutions, start assigning homes to everything. Don't remove labels or tags until you've determined that the storage solutions you've chosen will work. If you need more time or a different solution, don't fret. Most things can be returned. This step can take a bit of trial-and-error to get it right.

5. Label
One of the best ways to maintain an organized office space is to use labels to help you find your office supplies. Add adhesive or clip-on labels to magazine files, baskets, or boxes to really bring it home.

STYLE: CURATE YOUR INSPIRING OFFICE

An office can be a place you avoid because it means paying bills and answering emails, but it can also foster creativity, help you to reach your potential, and inspire you to share your gifts with the world. When I think about what holds so many of us back, it's the inability to move forward, finish what we started, and believe in our ability to achieve our dreams. But when you are knee-deep in clutter and your home is distracting rather than supporting you, it's natural to stay stuck.

White mixed with an additional color or texture makes both the space and items stand out.

▷ START HERE

1. Complete worksheet 3 (on page 153)

Imagine you, living your best life. What if it all started with a blank slate, a clear desk, and a clear mind? The thing is, I've seen it happen. That screenplay you want to write, business you want to start, charity you want to build—it's all possible and it can start now. Setting up your space to support your success is the first step. What styling elements can you add to infuse your workspace with intention now, so you can be in alignment with the life you want later?

2. Upgrade your basics

Think outside the storage box by combining form and function. You can find some great paper storage solutions at your neighborhood office supply shop, but you may also be surprised to find more stylish options at your favorite home goods, furniture, and even clothing stores, too.

> **PRO TIP:** Whether you are replacing your pens with a pretty upgrade or your magazine files with a new collection, use a cohesive, simple color theme for basic items throughout your space. When in doubt, white works out. If color is too bold, opt for whites. They can be mixed and matched or streamlined for optimal simplicity.

3. Mix materials

One of my favorite tips for an inspiring office that's simple rather than sterile is to mix materials. If bright white files make your heart sing, add in a few vintage finds or some natural materials to add texture. Sustainable alternatives to plastic, like paper, glass, wood, and wire, can elevate your space with depth and texture.

Personalize your office with pretty labels and cohesive bins to keep you inspired.

4. Display the picture worth a thousand words

For the purposes of this challenge, print and put up one inspirational photo that speaks to your heart and reminds you of where you're headed and your ultimate potential. Maybe you will choose a photo of your grandmother who paved the way for you to be the woman you are today, your brilliant boss bestie who reminds you of what's possible, or the mountain you climbed when you thought it was all just dream. What are the thousand words you need to hear today?

5. Rethink your walls

From wallpaper to gallery walls or a simple coat of paint, you can transform your space with just a touch of intentional love. Color is a powerful tool that stimulates our subconscious mind.

> **PRO TIP:** Explore some of my favorite paints and wallpapers from permanent to temporary in the Resource Guide on page 126.

6. Invest in form and function

There is nothing more important for any office, particularly a home office, than a comfortable, ergonomic chair and a beautiful functional desk (with storage). If you can't work comfortably, you're sabotaging your flow. There are great options out there, but make sure to look for office accessories that meld both form and function.

Resist the urge to cover every surface, allowing the eye and the mind to rest.

CHAPTER 9

PAPER

When I encounter a giant paper pile, it's rarely the result of hoarding or any real systemic issue. Paper clutter is a slow, sneaky, seemingly harmless beast (what's the harm in keeping one more receipt?) until you realize it's been killing you softly. Over time, if you don't cut the head off the snake, prepare for death by a thousand papercuts. One day you're innocently saving coupons, and the next you find yourself digging out of a grave filled with supporting tax documents from 1985 and three-inch thick catalogs you can't seem to part with.

Let's not forget the bills, the kids' homework, doctor's receipts, and everything else in between. Organizing the overflow of paper in your life and home may seem like a daunting task, but with the right tools, a little direction, and a few new healthy habits, you can gain control of those pesky paper piles.

TOP CLUTTER CULPRITS

Though we are rapidly moving toward a paperless world, paper is not yet a thing of the past. Do you spend more than ten minutes a day searching for papers that you need in pinch? The truth is, if you take the time now to get your papers organized and set up a few simple systems to keep your active paper flow on point, you'll save time and probably money in the long run (late fees anyone?). The following five paper clutter culprits may ring a bell, but here are five easy tips to implement right now:

Piles to file

Paper piles are everywhere. They're scattered around the house. They're in the kitchen and on or near the fridge. They rest by the front door and under your bed. They pile up against walls and on the floor and in the car and probably in the depths of your purse.

> **PRO TIP:** Decide now where your paper zones will be. Office and entry? Entry and garage? Only in your office? Keep paper clutter to a minimum by always and immediately putting paper in those designated zones. It will make processing your papers much easier if they always land where they should (not your floor, the kitchen counter, or some random drawer).

Way too much mail

We check the mail every day, and yet we waste valuable energy sorting through it only to get one or two envelopes that need our attention. In fact, almost 50 percent of your mail is junk that someone else decided should be important to you. Check out the Resource Guide on page 126 for links to unsubscribe from mailings, ads, and catalogs.

PRO TIP: When you take the envelopes out of the mailbox, immediately recycle any envelopes, ads, catalogs, and flyers that you don't need or that are not aligned with your goals. Keep a recycling bin or a divided recycling and shredding bin by your front door.

Fear of going paperless

We all fear change. People are hard-wired for comfort and familiarity and are not likely to change without a little kick in the pants.

PRO TIP: Go paperless. There is no better way to face your fears, go green, and get rid of paper clutter. Keep a running list in your notebook or digital note-taking app of any incoming mail that you can unsubscribe to. Sign up for paperless bank statements and bills the next time you get them in the mail. I promise, this will not only save you time and space, but also free you of the daily drain of an overstuffed mailbox.

Paper paralysis

One reason why we hang onto paper is that we're not sure what we need to keep or for how long. We get stuck, so we keep everything for that "someday, maybe."

PRO TIP: Refer to the checklist at the end of this chapter to determine how long you need to keep your important papers. The list will give you an idea of what you can let go of now.

The someday fallacy

Some people like me are more tactile than others, preferring to hold a book in their hands than read online. But just because you're more visual doesn't mean you need to keep papers you don't love, need, or use. Don't save the instruction pamphlet on how to assemble your IKEA desk in case it falls

apart and you'll have to reassemble it one day because that day may never come.

PRO TIP: Commit to recycling anything you can find easily online, especially if it is something you'll rarely access. I'm talking about manuals, instructions, phone books, and anything you can find with a two-minute Google search. Honestly, it's going to be one time in ten years when you'll need it.

GET MOTIVATED!

You don't have to see the entire staircase to take the first step. If you are standing at the bottom of a mountain (of paper), just begin. One of the most rewarding feelings is taking piles of old paper to the recycling bin or shredder. There's really nothing I love more than watching my paperwork and paid-off bills run through the teeth of that machine. It's the ultimate catharsis. There is freedom on the other side, and once you set up a few systems, you'll be well-suited to process your paper like a pro.

SIMPLIFY: DECLUTTER YOUR PAPER PILE-UP

By now you've gathered all your paper piles, files, boxes, and bins into one area. If your collection is just too big to tackle at once, start with one box, pile, or filing cabinet. The process is the same as any organizational project in this book, with just a few new tools.

If you find a sentimental item (photo or memento), set it aside to be addressed in Chapter 10, Photos, on page 104 and Chapter 11, Mementos, on page 114.

PAPER STARTER KIT

- 3.5-inch colored file tabs
- 3.5-inch transparent hanging file tabs
- Binder Clips
- File Bin/File Box
- File Folders
- Hanging Files
- Label Maker
- Letter Opener
- Post-its
- Sharpie
- Sorting Bin Labels
- Sorting Bins

▷ **START HERE**

1. Complete worksheet 1 (on page 154)

Before starting each step in this process, identify the goals you have for your paper build-up. Think about why you want to get your papers organized and what it will feel like when you do. Perhaps you are ready to finally go paperless, maybe you want to set up a better workflow, or you've got a book to write on a desk that's covered in piles. Complete the worksheet for an exercise in intention-setting to motivate you and inspire your paper purge.

2. Set up your workspace

The categories for organizing paper are slightly different for paper than for space. Label your bins: Recycle, Shred, Digitize and To-Do, plus any additional categories that you'd like to consider.

PRO TIP: Keep your notebook at the ready, especially for paper sorting. If you come across any action items, like paying a bill or following up with an old credit inquiry, write it down as a to-do item. Keeping track in your notebook will ensure you don't skip a beat, but don't stop your flow to check off your list until you've completed processing all your paper.

3. Pull everything out and group like-with-like

When all your papers are gathered into one space, start with one manageable pile. I call this the paper pre-sort, where you'll create general, temporary categories with Post-its for each paper grouping you come across. Use the category list included in this chapter to determine what categories of items you have or create your own based on what you are working with. If you already have some pre-sorted paper categories, keep those together.

PRO TIP: Use your Post-its and Sharpies to label your hanging files as you create categories. Don't add any permanent labels at this point, just a general category to get you through the stack. You can add your final categories later once you see all the types of paper you have.

4. Process your paper

Discard, recycle, or shred any paper item that you do not love, need, or use. Work diligently through your paper piles, one stack at time. This may take several hours or multiple sessions. Set a timer and dive into your paper with commitment. If you stay focused, you can get through more in a few hours than you can do in a few years. Protect your identity and add anything with your name, address, phone number, social security, or medical information directly into the shredding bin.

> **PRO TIP:** If you are dealing with a large backlog of paper or you have papers that you need to access often, separate your files into three master categories: Active, Accessible, and Archive. This way you can easily access those files that you need to keep on your desktop or in a nearby cabinet.

5. Make active files

Active files are typically located on a desktop or wall pocket, and they are a landing spot for all current, incoming, and everyday paper files. Things like bills to pay or school notices to read are examples of active files. You can set up your active paper system however it makes sense to you. I've included a list of my go-to active files in the Resource Guide on page 126.

6. Make accessible files

Accessible files belong in your main filing system. This can be a box or filing cabinet depending on the size of your paper lot. Use the category list in this chapter as a guideline for setting up your accessible files.

7. Archive

Archive files include things like old statements that you don't need to access regularly, supporting tax documents that you still need to hold on to but don't need often, old property documents and legal files, plus anything you don't currently access.

8. Wrap up

Always allow at least one hour for this step. Once you have processed your papers, wrap up your work session by clearing away any trash, recycling, or shredding. If you are ready to move on, skip ahead to step 2, Streamline, or put away any items that have an

MEDITATE ON THIS: GOING PAPERLESS

If digitizing paper files is on your goal list (and I hope it is!), I'm here to help because I know it can be scary. I've asked you to dedicate a box to digitization as you process your papers: Put anything you come across that can be scanned and stored digitally into this box.

If it's not a high priority for you and going paperless simply isn't in your wheelhouse, stick with a filing system that will work for you. But if you're ready to take the paperless plunge, take advantage of the tools that can help get you there. Use Post-its to identify the papers you want to digitize and set them aside in the "Digitize" bin. You can do it yourself if your pile is small (Genius Scan, Evernote, and even your iPhone camera has simple tools you can use), but if you're looking at a large backlog, you may want to outsource this task. Try not to get hung up on the best digital storage because you can always transfer your files if you find something better. Just choose a digital system that works for you. Dropbox, Google Drive, and Box all serve the same purpose. Backing up to an external hard drive is also a good rule of thumb if you don't have, or want, cloud storage. For more resources and tips on digital organizing and going paperless, head to www.simplyspaced.com.

intuitive home and take notes in your notebook about any items that don't. Move any homeless items to a temporary landing zone.

> **PRO TIP:** If you have your own shredder, you can shred DIY style, or you can find a local vendor to do it for you. Many office supply stores also shred securely for a small fee. Take a deep breath and enjoy the cleared energy of your decluttered papers.

15 THINGS TO LET GO OF NOW

1. Supporting tax documents over seven years old
2. Statements you can get digitally
3. Catalogs and manuals you can find online
4. Old shopping receipts that are now verified by your statements
5. Expired coupons
6. Outdated invitations
7. Greeting cards with just a signature
8. Advertisements
9. Old business cards
10. Expired warranties
11. Travel brochures
12. Verified ATM slips
13. Newspapers and magazines over 2 months old
14. Pay stubs (after reconciling W-2)
15. Outdated stories about yourself

COMMON FILING CATEGORIES

- Academic
- Auto
- Educational
- Employment
- Financial
  - Banking
  - Credit
  - Investments
  - Loans
  - Retirement
- Health Records
  - Dental
  - Medical
- Home Records
  - Deeds
  - Design
  - Improvements
  - Inventories
  - Landscaping
  - Mortgage
  - Repairs
  - Warranties
- Household
- IDs
- Insurance
  - Disability
  - Health
  - Homeowner/Renter
  - Life
  - Motor Vehicle
  - Personal Liability
- Kids
- Legal
- Membership
- Personal
- Pet
- Taxes
- Utilities
- Work

Use temporary labels as you organize to have the flexibility to make changes.

TIME PERIODS FOR SAVING PAPER

Keep for 1–3 Months

- Utility bills (keep 3-7 years if deductable for business)
- Paid citations
- Receipts for minor purchases
- ATM and bank deposit slips

Keep for 1 Year

- Check registers
- Check statements
- Credit card statements
- Paycheck stubs
- Cancelled checks
- Monthly mortgage statements
- Expired insurance records
- Monthly bank statements

Keep for 7 Years

- Annual bank statements
- W-2 and 1099 forms
- Receipts for tax purposes (including business meal receipts and business utilities)
- Charitable donation receipts
- Disability records
- Unemployment income stubs
- Medical bills and claims

Keep Forever

- Tax returns
- Deeds, mortgages, and bills of sale
- Investment statements for each year
- Legal documents and important IDs: birth certificates, divorce and death certificates, marriage license, military discharge papers, social security cards, permanent life insurance policies, and passports
- Home improvement documentation and receipts
- Receipts for expensive purchases such as art, major appliances, furnishing, and jewelry (for warranty and insurance purposes)
- Wills
- Power of attorney designation
- Beneficiary directions
- Real estate certificates
- Car titles
- Current insurance policies
- Medical records
- Education records
- Pension plan records
- Retirement records

STREAMLINE: OPTIMIZE YOUR PAPER-PROCESSING SYSTEMS

With the excess and overflow out of the way, you are now ready to set up your paper processing stations and filing system. The purpose of this step is to improve efficiency and ease of access, so don't set yourself up for frustration later by overcomplicating your systems now. Think about where and how you want to process your papers moving forward to make your life easier.

▷ **START HERE**

1. Complete worksheet 2 (on page 155)
Use your worksheet to guide you through this process of refining your paper system. Identify what has and has not been working. Now that you have decluttered and identified your categories, think about what can be improved by optimizing storage.

2. Create zones
Whether you've landed on an entry setup to process and file or at a desk nestled in your office, I recommend keeping your paper stations limited to one or two areas of the house. First, identify your final landing spot for active, general, and archive files. Designate a shelf near your desk or mail station for your active files. If you have boxes of old statements or medical records, consider an area in an attic or garage that can house the archives.

> **PRO TIP:** Don't just limit your landing spots, but also limit your influx. I like to designate one magazine file for magazines and catalogs that I want to read. I rarely even get through that many, but I recycle and refresh monthly. This keeps me honest and my zone intact.

3. Maximize space
Once you've decided where you want to process and store paper and files, it's time to set up your ideal workstations to support your paper management. If you've been extremely diligent about your processing, you may be limited to one file box or maybe you need a filing cabinet. If your current system is working, it may just be a matter of filing. Make a list of any storage solutions you'll need to rework in your space. I recommend a file box, file sorter, or wall pocket to hold your active files. Next, you'll need a general file box or filing cabinet for your family and work files. Also think about purchasing some weather-tight bins to store

A "to file" box is perfect for papers to file at a later time.

archive files in an out-of-the-way spot like the basement, attic, garage, or suspended loft space.

> **PRO TIP:** Take measurements of drawers, cabinets, and any space where you'll need to store these files. Hire a handyperson if you need an extra shelf or could benefit from pullouts.

4. Implement storage solutions
Set up your paper stations with the optimal tools for your workflow. Think about ease of access and how you will maintain your systems. As with everything, if your solution doesn't work now, you can always switch it out later.

> **PRO TIP:** Set up an active desktop filing system (or use wall pockets) for your most current or everyday papers.

MY PERSONAL ACTIVE DESKTOP FILE INCLUDES:

To Process:
This is a landing spot for anything that I need to deal with: a stack of mail, a pile of paper I found hidden somewhere, a set of work documents I need to decode. I like to keep it off my desk, and I process it daily when I have some down time.

To Pay
This is for any bills that come through, an invoice left by the carpet cleaner, or another parking citation.

To Do
This is anything that needs my attention, but not immediately. Currently, it's the vitamins I want to order, a newsletter I'd like to read, and a follow-up notice from the vet. Once I've had a chance to look through these papers, I either take care of them right away or transfer the task to my digital to-do list.

To File
This is for everything I have already dealt with but don't need to file right away. I like to file my folder once it gets full so that I don't have to waste time with every individual piece of paper.

To Reference
I use this folder for invites, flyers, brochures, and current activities. I do have every intention of going to the Hollywood Bowl this year, so I'm keeping the brochure until I have some time to book tickets (you get the idea).

Taxes
I keep this file in my active file bin because it's an easy landing spot for tax-related documents for the current tax year. When I am done and my taxes are filed, they go into my accessible file system along with supporting tax documents from the last seven years.

5. Label

One of the best ways to maintain an organized paper system is to use labels to help you and your loved ones find files easily. Using broad categories (and only subdividing when necessary) will keep your system simple and uncomplicated. Remove your temporary labels and replace them with permanent labels. Refer to the common category list, or you can develop your own. There's no science to how to set yours up, it just needs to make sense to you.

> **PRO TIP:** Every professional organizer I know labels his or her files in one line rather than staggered. It's much more visually satisfying and easier to read and maintain. To separate labeled sections, you can divide them with a colorful hanging file or add a master tab in a single color to the front of each category.

By now all your paper filing systems should be set up. This is a good time to sit down with any to-dos, to pays, or additional filing items to wrap up your paper project. If you are largely reliant on paper, you can always move toward a paperless system later. Congratulations on making it this far and carry on to the next step for some styling tips to upgrade your paper systems and inspire you to maintain it. Let's not forget that life happens in the mess, but with systems thinking in place, you'll be back on track in no time.

STYLE: CURATE YOUR PAPER-PROCESSING STATION

Once you have all your papers decluttered and neatly filed away, it can be fun to style your paper processing station, so you are inspired to maintain them. Orderly paper files are incredibly empowering. It does not require a fancy system with hundreds of colored tabs and folders. In fact, if you ask me, the simpler and more streamlined, the better.

▷ START HERE

1. Complete worksheet 3 (on page 156)
Do you get excited about pretty files and fun labels, or do you prefer your paper systems simple and straightforward? Think about how you would like to see your paper files and what might inspire you to keep them organized.

2. Buy cohesive containers and paper files
I always recommend replacing mismatched functional storage with stylish containers and files if you are feeling overwhelmed and uninspired by your paper. A streamlined color palette will have a calming effect on your psyche. Color can be powerful, but it can also be a distraction. I say, leave your creative prowess to the key elements of the room—art, wallpaper, decor—and let your paper system blend into the space. When it comes to paper processing, which is an intrinsically overwhelming task, reducing distractions and creating a sense of Zen cohesion is a good thing.

3. Upgrade your labels
File boxes, magazine files, wall racks, and more can benefit from labels too. Label plates are surprisingly easy to find at most office supply stores. I use these on so many paper-related things to refresh the standard label.

> **PRO TIP:** Use handwritten labels. They are not only easy to make, but they bring a level of personalization into your workspace. If you like the look but don't have the skill, farm out this task to a friend with good penmanship.

4. Use 3.5-inch tabs
It's all in the details, right? How could something so simple be such an important styling tip? Well, try spelling "Betty's Retirement Plan" on a two-inch tab. Longer tabs are key to readability, which

equals maintainability. I honestly don't even know why they make the smaller ones.

5. Curate an inspiration board
The best way to manifest the life you want is to *look* at it every day. I am a huge fan of Pinterest and going paperless, but I also know the power of pinning in real life. There's nothing wrong with collecting inspiration, and you shouldn't have to shove it in a drawer only to forget about it later. If you are motivated by inspiring images, challenge yourself to curate just one board in your space to inspire and ignite your creativity.

CHAPTER 10

PHOTOS

Although we live in the digital age, there was a time when flipping through printed albums and stacks of 4 x 6-inch prints was the norm. Do you remember the days of one-hour photo processing? You could get a manicure while waiting for your roll of film to develop and then go home to slap your prints into an album with stickers and glitter glue. Today, we take, store, and experience photos much differently. We can take hundreds of photos a day, and most of us don't print photos at all.

For those of you who still have boxes and bins of cherished memories stacked away that you're looking to preserve for years to come, this chapter is for you. I'm not trying to be a Debbie Downer, but considering all the fires, floods, other natural disasters, and the tumultuous, unpredictable state of our world, organizing and saving printed photos has been top of mind for many of my clients as of late.

In the last two years, I lost my two beloved grandmothers. Because of the close relationship I had with these cherished matriarchs and my passion for family history, I had made it a priority to curate and organize all their photos before they had passed. Because I had these images at my disposal, I was able to put together a meaningful tribute for these women that everyone greatly appreciated. As hard as it was to say goodbye, it felt amazing to be able to honor their memories with slideshows of their lives at each of their ceremonies. Even though it took me a long time

to get my personal collection organized, I knew it was imperative to gather and organize *their* legacies, which were slowly degrading in old shoe boxes and yellowing albums. As an archivist in the art department and having worked in film for many years, this archival process came naturally to me. But I realize that many people think of organizing their photos as a tedious chore (and there's nothing glamorous about it), which is why I'm passionate about helping you start and finish this challenge.

If turning your printed photos into a manageable and accessible collection seems overwhelming, follow the steps in this chapter to get started. There are simple ways to get your photos gathered, organized, and backed up quickly and efficiently.

TOP CLUTTER CULPRITS

Most people have printed photos somewhere in the house, but the biggest problem is when you have printed photos *everywhere*. It makes sense to have albums and framed photos, but if you don't have these images backed up, it's easy to lose track of them. To identify the major photo missteps I see most often, here are five photo clutter culprits, plus five tips to implement now:

No permanent landing spot
Your photos are stored in boxes in the garage or stuffed in albums in the attic. There are bins under your bed. You keep most of them stored away in the basement, while a select few are framed on display. You've got albums on the shelf, files in your office, and oh, wait, your aunt just sent you her entire legacy in a shoe box. Now what?

Album-free for all

I get it, you love your albums. But how often do you look at them? Did you know that 70 percent of the albums we find in client homes are not acid free? That means your photos are dying a slow death—and those yellow pages are a telltale sign. I'm not suggesting that you get rid of all your albums, just the ones that are old, falling apart, and yellow.

Befuddled by backup

In the digital age, if you have a printed photo, it's likely you have a digital version somewhere too. Or do you? It really depends on what year the photo was taken. You may have that photo as a negative, or maybe it's on your now defunct Myspace page. Or perhaps you don't have digital versions, so that heap of photos really does need a backup.

Inherited memories

Time and time again I've seen my clients hold onto old collections they inherited, even when they had no idea who most of the people in the pictures were. I'm not suggesting you throw the entire collections away, but if your cherished loved ones are buried in a pile of unidentifiable history, collect and scan the most important ancestral images that have likely started to degrade.

Sentimental paralysis

You may not be ready to face your photos. Maybe you've got too many ties to old memories and it's an emotional burden that's just too big to bear. Truth be told, I did great with my ancestral photos, but when it came time to organize my own collection, the process was just too much for me. I gathered all my photos, sat down with Nancy, our beloved and trustworthy photo organizer, and passed off the project to get it done.

GET MOTIVATED!

When I talk about organizing your photos, I'm really talking about preserving your memories and legacy. The key is to enter this project with joy and presence. It's quite possible that you'll enjoy your photos more during this process than ever again, so be present. Getting organized with grace and self-love is pivotal to your success. Shift the energy of your "why" from "because I need to" to "because I want to."

PHOTOS

SIMPLIFY: DECLUTTER YOUR PILES OF PRECIOUS PICTURES

The first step in any organizational project is to declutter and downsize, and we'll do the same thing with printed photos. Gather all your photos, albums, scrapbooks, negatives, and photo media into one space. You'll need a few new tools to organize your photos. You can put together a mini photo-organizing kit with the tools below.

TOOLS:

- Notebook
- Pen
- Sharpie
- Post-its
- Trash Bags
- Rubber Bands
- Sorting Bins (four to five)

OPTIONAL EXTRAS:

- Dental Floss
- White Cotton Gloves
- Photo Pencil
- Index Cards
- Photo Box

▷ **START HERE**

1. Complete worksheet 1 (on page 157)

Before starting each step in this process, get clear on the goals you have for your photos. Think about why you want to get them organized and what it will feel like when you do. Identify what you'd like to accomplish by getting your photos organized. Do you want to create a family tree? A slideshow for a loved one? Printed photo books or sharable albums? Get clear on your intentions before starting this project and let them guide and motivate your progress. Complete the worksheet to identify your photo organizing goals and to connect with your "why."

2. Set up your workspace

Use your standard tool kit as referenced on pages 9–10. Label your bins: Donate, Trash, Recycle, and To Digitize. If you have sensitive photos or documents in your photo pile, you may want to include a shredding bin.

> **PRO TIP:** Create a family timeline with important dates like marriage, birth, big events, and memorable moments like that year you had braces and pink hair.

3. Pull everything out and group like-with-like

Gather all your photos and organizing tools into one area where you can spread out. Begin to sort your collection, grouping like-with-like and separating printed photos from other forms of media like slides and film. Separate out sentimental items, and any non-photo items (mementos are addressed in Chapter 11 on page 114).

PHOTO AND MEDIA TYPES

Non-digital	Digital
• Printed Photos	• Digital Photos
• Slides	• SD Cards
• Negatives	• Thumb and Hard Drives
• VHS Tapes	• CDS/DVDs
• Film	• Cameras

Before separating photos from their negatives, number and label the corresponding grouping. That way you can choose to digitize one or the other and not both.

4. Process your photos and categorize

Donate, discard, or recycle any photos that you do not love, need, or care to revisit. I'm talking about duplicates, blurry images, and throwaways. If you have albums you want to scan but keep intact, create notes about the nature of the photos in them according to your category list. Use the Common Photo Categories list, opposite, to start making sense of your photo collection and sort your photos into piles using Post-its. Once you have determined your categories, keep them together with a Post-it and rubber band. It can be helpful to go back and sort through each category so that your images are chronological within each grouping, but don't get caught up in the minutia.

> **PRO TIP:** If you want to cut clutter and rid yourself of photo degrading, carefully remove photos from old, yellowing albums (dental floss helps with delicate removal). Take a photo if you want to remember the album, and then recycle the non-acid-free pages and envelopes. You can donate any mismatched albums.

5. Wrap up

Always allow at least one hour for this step. Once you have processed your photos, wrap up your work session by clearing away any trash and recycling from your workspace. If you are ready to move on, skip ahead to step 2, Streamline, or put away any items that have an intuitive home and take notes in your notebook about any items that don't. Move any homeless items to a temporary landing zone.

> **PRO TIP:** Store your photos in a safe area of the home. Attics, garages, and basements are not ideal locations for storing your photos. Insects and rodents love paper, so keep pictures stored in archival albums and bins. Take a deep breath and enjoy the cleared energy of your decluttered photos.

We always recommend categorizing your printed photos before digitizing to save time and money. It's much easier to scan photos in pre-organized groups. Unless you are working with a professional photo organizer, sending unsorted photos to a scanning company will only give you another digital mess to deal with.

Broad categories will keep you from feeling overwhelmed as you watch your photo piles grow. My photos are organized like this: early childhood, high school, college, grad school, and so on.

COMMON PHOTO CATEGORIES

Person

- Mom
- Dad
- Brother
- Sister

Family

- Mom's Side
- Dad's Side
- Ancestors

Friends

Major Events

- Childbirth
- Bar and Bat Mitzvah
- Graduations
- Year Abroad
- Wedding
- Honeymoon
- New Home

Theme or Holiday

- Anniversaries
- Birthdays
- Christmas
- Halloween
- Hanukkah
- Vacations
- Sports
- Work Events

Time/Date

- Early Childhood
- Middle School
- High School
- College
- Graduate School
- Pre-Marriage
- Marriage
- Kids

Oversized

15 THINGS TO LET GO OF NOW

1. Duplicates
2. Bad or blurry photos
3. Similar photos
4. Unflattering photos
5. Yellowing albums (non-acid-free)
6. Mismatched albums and containers
7. Envelopes
8. Photos of people you don't know
9. Bad memory photos
10. Redundant locations
11. Unidentifiable scenery photos
12. Unused film
13. Old cameras you won't use
14. Negatives that have been scanned or developed
15. Excuses

STREAMLINE: OPTIMIZE YOUR PHOTO COLLECTION

The process of streamlining your photo collection is different from the other projects we've tackled so far in this book. Follow the steps below to digitize your photo collection and organize it for safekeeping.

Organize your photos by chronology, event, theme, or person. There is no perfect way, only the way that makes sense to you.

▷ **START HERE**

1. Complete worksheet 2 (on page 158)
Use your worksheet to guide you through this process to refine your photo system. Identify what has and has not been working. Now that you have decluttered and identified your categories, think about what can be improved by optimizing storage.

2. Double check your collection
You can be as precise as you need to be but keep your goals in mind. If you need a complex and detailed chronology and family history, you'll need to do some research and look for clues like dates. If your goal is to get your collection organized and backed up as quickly as possible, you may want to do the best you can to get the photos ordered, but remember that general categories will help you find the photos you are looking for regardless of their exact order.

> **PRO TIP:** Order your groupings in a relative chronology. For example, start with early childhood: infant photos, toddler, kindergarten, and so on. This way, you will get a scanned collection that's easy to navigate.

3. Scan your photos
People scan their photos because they want to preserve their memories over time. I highly recommend outsourcing this step to save a lot of time, effort, and money.

> **PRO TIP:** If you outsource the scanning, make sure your photos are scanned at a minimum 600 dpi and 3,000 dpi for negatives and slides. And check that your scanning partner will scan the photos into your pre-sorted categories.

4. Identify and cull your favorite photos
Once you have your photos scanned, you'll likely enjoy flipping through your photos in digital form. It's a good idea to flag, star, or highlight your favorites so that you can begin to think about what you want to do with them. Perhaps you'll create a gallery wall, slideshow, or a personalized video that takes your college bestie down memory lane before you send her down the aisle. Once your photos are digitized, there are infinite possibilities, including creating and sharing albums.

5. Back up your collection
If you're having your photos scanned, it's likely they will be delivered by a link to download or an external drive, and it's up to you to back up and store your files. I keep my personal collection on a hard drive in a safe and on the cloud and on my desktop.

> **PRO TIP:** I recommend backing up your photos in three different places like a cloud, external hard drive, and safety deposit box. I've seen hard drives give out and libraries lost, so in this case, more is more. The Resource Guide on page 126 has a variety of back-up options.

Acid-free photo boxes conserve physical photos.

6. Implement storage

Once your photos are scanned, backed-up, and saved, you'll need to store any physical copies in professional-grade, acid-free photo boxes to preserve their health over time. Use weathertight containers for an added level of protection in questionable spaces. You may decide that once your collection is backed up, you no longer need the physical copies, but most of my clients keep them.

> **PRO TIP:** Keep all oversized photos stored together in their own category. Most oversized photos don't fit in your standard photo boxes, so get a separate one for this type of collection.

7. Label

Once you've divided all your photos into storage containers, label the outsides of the boxes according to the broad categories and subdivide within. This is your opportunity to reassess your categories and move things around as needed.

> **PRO TIP:** Add any newly printed photos to your existing photo collection. If you pull photos from your collection, make sure to file them back where you found them.

MEDITATE ON THIS: THE MEANING OF PHOTOS

A picture tells a thousand words. If our home reflects our life, what stories does it tell? If your walls could talk, what would they say? In any home, a photo is a remarkable way to pay homage to your loved ones. Filling your empty walls with your adventures is an opportunity to celebrate and express gratitude for the life you lead. If you want to see a child get excited about something novel and special, give her a printed photo of herself or display it on the wall.

Physical photos ground us and connect us to the here and now, a fleeting experience in the digital age. With so many ways to stylishly frame and display photos, it's easier than ever to paint our story across the walls and instantly bring warmth, life, and energy to our home.

STYLE: CURATE YOUR PHOTO COLLECTION

Once your printed photos are organized, backed up and ready to share with the world, there are infinite ways to display them with style. On the walls or on a shelf, as a gift or for yourself, think outside the box and surround your loved ones with the fruits of your labor. Photos are meant to be shared and tell your story, so have fun, get creative, and enjoy. Here are my best tips for styling your photos.

A photo gallery prominently showcases your most memorable moments.

▷ **START HERE**

1. Complete worksheet 3 (on page 158)
Think about how you'd like to view your photos and what you'd ultimately like to have done with them. Are you ready to print and frame, create a gallery wall, or just share with family? Use your worksheet to guide you and the tips below for inspiration.

2. Curate a gallery wall
Update your walls to align with your present. There are so many resources that can make

gallery wall creation a breeze. As my friend and home energy healer Dorena Kohrs says, "don't expect your adult children living at home to act like adults if the only photos you have up are of them as babies."

> **PRO TIP:** Consider adding some cherished mementos to your gallery wall to mix things up. Framebridge is my favorite for framing ticket stubs, magazine articles, and photos alike. They even have pre-designed gallery layouts, plus design experts available to make it even easier to get your photos up.

Photo books not only neatly preserve your favorite photos but also make for great gifts.

3. Create photo books

Photo books are number one on the list of most-requested items on the Simply Spaced menu and we have so much fun creating them. They look great on the shelf, they make memorable gifts, they bring the family together and they are a lasting, clutter-free reminder of the beautiful memories made by families. There are so many incredible resources for photobooks out there, but my go-tos are Mixbook and Artifact Uprising.

4. Style your shelves with photos

One of the best ways to personalize any space is by adding photos. We connect to faces more than anything else and if you want to make your home feel more inviting, don't be afraid to show your face.

5. Create a shareable album, video, or slideshow

One of the best parts of digitizing your printed photos is seeing them on a screen for the first time. I love watching clients flip through their photos on a computer or flat screen after only ever seeing them as a 4 x 6 inches. High school reunion coming up? A wedding or special event? Videos and slideshows are a great way to commemorate your photo organization process and they are so very fun to share.

Grandma Betty on the boardwalk.

My Grandma Mary in the Military.

Grandma Colleen at my Great-Grandma's graduation.

CHAPTER 11

MEMENTOS

For many of my clients, sentimental collections, mementos, and memorabilia are a pain point, because what may be trash to one person is a treasure to another. So how do we navigate this uncharted territory? How do we cohabitate when what's special to one person is total rubbish to another? It's all about the systems, especially when it comes to sentimental items.

Yesterday, a cleaning crew did a deep clean and accidentally threw out some of my old lab drawings my mom had recently found. While momentarily saddened (I wanted to be a scientific illustrator once), my current job has taught me a lot about non-attachment. However, it hit my mom like a ton of bricks.

My husband likes Kobe Bryant paraphernalia, movie memories, his grandfather's watch, and shoes. Beyond that, he's not the sentimental type. It doesn't mean his traveling campsite is any smaller, but it makes one area of our lives a little easier. I, on the other hand, come from a long line of collectors. When my grandmother died, she had rooms filled floor-to-ceiling with boxes of memories, treasures, clothes, and art—one hundred years of life manifested into reality (and no editing). I fall somewhere in the middle, inspired and attached to special memories, but uniquely adept at editing out the non-essential after years of clutter clearing.

When it comes to organizing special mementos, you need to follow some basic guidelines and master a few new habits to set up a systematic, curated, and stress-free home that's full of memories and free of clutter. And with the right setup and awareness, your household can cohabitate a little more harmoniously.

TOP CLUTTER CULPRITS

I've developed a process for collecting, storing, and displaying cherished memories. It is one of the most significant things I do as a professional organizer. Since we are all individuals, it's important to honor the needs of those we live with, even if they differ from our own. To keep your sanity and reduce the overwhelm, I've got a few hacks to keep those precious memories in order. Let's first identify the top sentimental clutter causes.

We don't identify mementos as mementos

One reason we deal with clutter is that many of us have no guidelines for determining what's special and what's garbage. We are even worse at determining this for other people. A memento, by definition, is an object or souvenir kept as a reminder of a person, place, thing, or event. Teach your family this, and teach them young. If they understand that there's a way to define and categorize special objects, they will be better prepared to start differentiating between what they like and what they love.

Everything is special

If everything is special, nothing is special. Many of us cherish every memory without identifying the stand-out moments or life-changing experiences. A card with just a signature doesn't hold the same weight as a letter with a handwritten, heartfelt message.

Sentimental self-sabotage

You feel like you must hold onto everything, and so you do. You feel guilty throwing out a crayon drawing with your child's name on it; you save every movie stub because someday you will put them in a scrapbook.

The "someday, maybe" fallacy

You think that someday your kids are going to want all their stuff, or worse, you think someday your kids will want all *your* stuff. You've got so many scrapbooks to make.

Collector chaos

From toy cars and action figures to rocks, gems, and signage, I've seen it all. For the purposes of this chapter, I am making a clear distinction between a collection and a memento, and I think it is important for you to differentiate too. For one person, an item may seem like just another meaningless trinket, but for another it could be a part of a bigger collection. Simply put, a collection is something important to its owner that should be honored and respected, even if you don't see the value in it yourself.

GET MOTIVATED!

Keepsakes or mementos are how we honor, appreciate, and remember the special moments, events, and people in our lives. All of us have varying attachments and levels of sentimentality that can change as we move through various seasons of our lives. Emotions, fears, life events, and other people have a huge impact on how and what we save. This is why it is so important not to make decisions about sentimental items for other people. If you are a parent, or stepparent, or roommate, it's your right to ask your living partners to set limits.

MEMENTOS

SIMPLIFY: DECLUTTER YOUR MEMENTO AND MEMORABILIA MESS

Start this step when you have gathered your mementos and sentimental items in one place. Follow my three-step system to declutter and downsize your mementos and set yourself and your family up with a yearly memento system to keep clutter under control. If you don't yet have a backlog of mementos (lucky you), skip to step 2, Streamline, to establish your new memento system.

▷ **START HERE**

1. Complete worksheet 1 (on page 159)
Before starting each step in this process, identify the goals you have for your sentimental items. Think about why you want to get them organized and what it will feel like when you do. Think about how you and the people you live with operate. If there are several sentimental people in your home, you'll likely need memento boxes, storage, and an archive to keep it all. Take a minute to think about why you want to get your sentimental items organized and how much you'll want to keep over the next decade or more. Complete the worksheet as an exercise in getting in alignment.

Begin by gathering your mementos and keeping only what you love and has special meaning.

2. Set up your workspace
Use your standard tool kit on pages 9–10. Label your bins: Donate, Trash, Recycle, Other Room, and Archive, plus any additional categories that you'd like to consider.

> **PRO TIP:** Set up at least one designated bin as needed for each member of your family. Depending on the amount of space you have and the volume of your sentimental items, you may need additional storage boxes or bins.

3. Pull everything out and group like-with-like
Gather your memento bins in one place. Hopefully, as you've moved through your home, you've collected mostly everything into one area. Use the category list in this chapter to determine what categories of items you have. There is no science to how you categorize, as long as it makes sense to you.

> **PRO TIP:** If you are sorting through multiple boxes of sentimental items that include photos or media, separate anything you want to digitize and backup. Refer to Chapter 10 on page 104 for how to organize your printed photo and media collections.

4. Process your mementos and categorize
Donate, discard, or recycle any mementos that you do not love, need, or care to revisit. As you reminisce and sort through your items, ask yourself which items have meaning and which items simply do not. What may have once seemed paramount, may now seem insignificant. Don't be afraid to let things go. It's quite possible that you will enjoy your items more during this sorting process than ever again.

> **PRO TIP:** Take a picture of any item you like but are willing to discard. It's okay to honor and revere an item by letting it go. Even the most precious mementos are just memories if they are beyond repair, eaten by moths, or soiled with mold.

5. Wrap up

Always allow at least one hour for this step. Once you have processed your mementos, wrap up your work session by clearing away any trash, recycling, donations, and shredding from your workspace. If you are ready to move on, skip ahead to step 2, Streamline, or add temporary labels to your piles or bins and find a temporary, safe home for them. Take notes in your notebook about any items you need to find storage for.

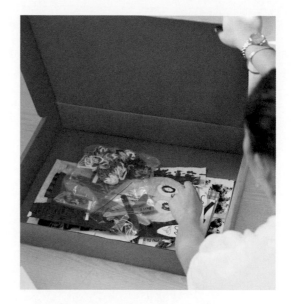

> **PRO TIP:** This is a great time to share some of your newfound memories with friends and family. Once they go back in a bin, it's unlikely they will be appreciated again for some time. Take a deep breath and enjoy the cleared energy of your decluttered mementos.

15 THINGS TO LET GO OF NOW

1. Overflow trophies from childhood
2. Valueless sports memorabilia
3. Cards without a meaningful note
4. Redundant kid art
5. School advertisements
6. Giant dioramas and posters (take a picture)
7. Old stuffed animals
8. Items that are no longer meaningful
9. Moldy keepsakes
10. Moth-eaten clothing
11. Reminders of past traumas
12. Extra invitations to your wedding (keep three)
13. Old travel brochures
14. Anything that makes you feel sad, angry, or anxious
15. Pleasing everyone

COMMON MEMENTO CATEGORIES

Person/Family
- Ancestors
- Billy
- Dad
- Jo
- Mom

Friends

Major Events
- Bar and Bat Mitzvah
- Graduations
- Honeymoon
- Wedding
- Year Abroad

Theme or Holiday
- Anniversaries
- Birthdays
- Christmas
- Halloween
- Sports

- Vacations
- Work

Time/Date
- College
- Early Childhood
- Graduate School
- High School
- Kids
- Marriage
- Middle School
- Pre-Marriage

Other
- Correspondence
- Sports Memorabilia
- Sentimental Clothing
- Awards and Recognitions
- School Work

STREAMLINE: OPTIMIZE MEMENTO STORAGE

Between kids' art and toys, homework, movies stubs, and rock collections, sentimental items can build back up again fast without the right systems. Here are my best tips for streamlining your photos.

▷ **START HERE**

1. Complete worksheet 2 (on page 160)

Use your worksheet to guide you through this process to refine your memento system. Identify what has and has not been working. Now that you have decluttered and identified your categories, think about what can be improved by optimizing storage.

2. Create zones

Identify a landing spot for long-term storage of your mementos as well as a home for collecting mementos throughout the year.

> **PRO TIP:** When I'm working with clients who have children, I designate one bin or box for each family member at the start of every school year.

3. Maximize Space

To keep your memento influx under control and sentimental clutter at bay over the long haul, purchase a few large bins for each family member. Setting a limit now will save you a lot of stress in the long run.

4. Implement Storage Solutions

Add a school year box for each family member, fill it up throughout the year, and edit things out when it reaches capacity. At the end of the year, edit your mementos and keep only those items that still feel special. Add the keepers to your permanent bin.

> **PRO TIP:** Use Artkive to create a book of your children's art and special projects. They send a pre-labeled box to your house and make it easy to turn your kids' art into a book the whole family will love.

5. Label

Label your memento boxes by person, event, or time period. I like to designate one box for each child that is labeled with the school year, "Holly 2019–2020," for example. You may want to include who, what, when, and notes on contents if you are labeling a memento bin to be archived.

Do you want to eventually make a book for each child, maybe for each year, or for each elementary school grade? Decide now and make it easier later.

STYLE: CURATE YOUR MEMENTOS

In many ways, the home itself is an oversized time capsule of our memories. If a stranger entered your home tomorrow, without having much context or insight, it would tell your story. What would it say? There is power in understanding that our external dwelling is a representation of who we are. What we see in our homes every day—consciously or unconsciously—either supports the narrative we have in our hearts or pulls us further from that manifestation.

The opportunity in this awareness is to shift your mindset, focusing on the things that make you feel good. I believe that a timeless room honors a piece of your history, reflects where you are now, and lays out a canvas for your future. This is precisely why I love to style with curated and meaningful mementos.

▷ **START HERE**

1. Complete worksheet 3 (on page 160)
What would you like to see happen with your mementos? Do you want to frame a few, take photos, or create a time capsule? Use the worksheets for this chapter as a guide for inspiration.

2. Display three things you love
Earlier, I spoke about choosing three things in each room to display. A spin on this styling hack is to use your favorite mementos. Chose three favorite items, like a child's art work, a playbill from your favorite musical, or a cherished toy from your childhood to put on display around the house. Bookshelves, walls, and dressers are all fair game.

3. Create art and memory books
More than anything, my clients love the photo and memory books I create for them. You can take a photo of your favorite item and insert it into a book.

> **PRO TIP:** Mixbook is my favorite photo album software for ease of use. I can add blank pages for special mementos to slip inside and merge them with their photo counterparts.

Artkive is my favorite way to easily keep and preserve kids' art and mementos for posterity. These books make great gifts and cut down on storage needs.

Curate your mementos with reason and purpose.

I like to keep memento boxes for each member of the family in an easy to access area, archiving the contents at the end of each school year.

4. Frame special objects
Add your favorite memories to a gallery wall to mix it up and make it more dynamic. I've framed everything from magazines and ticket stubs to jerseys and toy cars.

5. Make a memory blanket
Blankets can be made from old college tee-shirts, high school sports jerseys, kids' outgrown favorites, or even designer duds. A memory blanket is the perfect way to honor a few sentimental items without having to keep the entire lot.

> **PRO TIP:** Once you've processed your mementos and identified the special keepsakes, try using an online framing company like Framebridge to get the project done without leaving the house.

FINAL WRAP UP

As I write my conclusion, I am overwhelmed by excitement that my words and ideas can come into the world this year. I recently Facetimed with my husband, who is working in New Mexico, and we both had a moment of true gratitude for all the good in our lives. Even though we couldn't be together, we both feel passionately committed to and excited about where our lives have landed us in the most unexpected and beautiful way. Writing this book is the best gift I could receive, and my husband has experienced similar gratitude, having recently celebrated his birthday while producing his second television show. But let's be honest, his real gift was six new pairs of shoes from his friends.

So, here we are, husband and wife, trying for a child, excited to lean into the future, and cohabitating in the same condo we started out in over nine years ago. Looking around, it's interesting to think we moved here believing this place needed a lot of love and that we would only stay for a year. But then we fell in love with our quiet neighborhood and realized that we had about as much space as we could manage and by staying put, we'd be able to save money and focus on our businesses. Keeping up with the Joneses was impossible anyway, especially

with the high cost of living in L.A., so we whole-heartedly embraced the idea of making this place work for us, and it has. Now I can honestly say that my home supports me, and I feel like our little corner of the world has served us well.

I have learned that there's no reason *not* to love the home you live in now. One thing I learned in production design is that if you can turn a cardboard box into a magical fairy forest, you can turn a four-walled space into anything you can imagine. My hope is that you take some of the tips, ideas, and resources in this book and turn them into inspiration. Take a tip, take a page, take a chapter, or take on the "Year of Clear" challenge. The process begins with clearing the clutter and evolves by optimizing space. Soon enough, your home becomes a reflection of your heart.

ABOUT THE AUTHOR

With a master's degree from the prestigious American Film Institute and a background in production design, Monica cultivated a curiosity for efficient space, design, time management, and the power of organizational systems early in her career. Her highly sought-after company, Simply Spaced, includes in-home professional organizing services, as well as branded content creation for organizing and lifestyle companies including iDesign, The Container Store, Evernote, Cuyana, Caavo, Winc, Artkive, and others.

Monica is a member of the National Association of Productivity and Organizing Professionals (NAPO), as well as the Association of Personal Photo Organizers (APPO), and The Art Directors Guild (ADG). Her work has been featured across print and digital media including *Better Homes & Gardens*, Apartment Therapy, Livestrong.org, Brit & Co, MindBodyGreen.com, Domino.com, *Flea Market* magazine, Who What Wear, NEST, and *You* magazine. She was a two-time guest on *The Influencer Podcast* with Julie Solomon and guest contributor on the *Style Matters* podcast.

MONICA LEED is an innovator, art director, and principal founder of the professional organizing company Simply Spaced, focused on organizing for the creative mind. She is a leading expert, speaker, and author. With an A-list celebrity client list and a roster that includes influencers, industry executives, and high-performing entrepreneurs, she has spent the past seven years developing her methodology to clear the clutter and style homes for optimal performance. Monica has helped hundreds of clients get organized and inspired, from the inside out.

What Monica found missing from the newly popularized decluttering movement was any mention of style. But it's her passion for curating inspiring spaces that tell a story that motivates her work with clients today. She believes everyone deserves to live in a beautiful and joy-filled home that inspires creativity, calm, and purpose. As a creative herself, Monica is a firm believer that everyone has the ability to "learn to think like an organizer" by adopting the tools, tricks, and mindset of the pros. Her want for everyone is the ability to transform their home into a haven that supports them to live their best life.

ACKNOWLEDGMENTS

THANK YOU, first and foremost, to my husband Jeff. Your laughs and love continue to make the impossible possible. Thank you to my dear friend Jen Giorgio Das, whose guidance and heart got this book off the ground. Thank you to Holly Christiano, Simply Spaced Operations Manager and house mom, for sticking with me through this crazy adventure: you are a unicorn. Thank you to my incredibly talented Graphic Designer Chloe White, Web Designer Lexi Parker, to my Attorney Jamie Lieberman, and to my mom, Julie, whose love and support has been unwavering.

Thank you to the amazing photographers that contributed their time and hearts to this project: Amanda Proudfit, Tess Alexander, Kara Coleen, Marisa Vitale, Stephanie Day, and Daniel Hennessy. Thank you to my service partners and gurus Nancy and Gary McFarland, Michal Cohen, Lauren Rashap, Adrienne Masi, Cari Butler, Maria Mesick, Rayne Parvis, and Dorena Kohrs.

A special thank you to the team at Quarto Publishing, including my Editor John Foster, Managing Editor Cara Donaldson, Creative Director Laura Drew, and Group Publisher Rage Kindelsperger, for your faith in me throughout this process.

I would not be here today without the love, support, and encouragement of my peers and professional community. A special thank you to Melody Mesick, Beth Penn, Julia de'Caneva, Kitt Fife, Joni Weiss, Shira Gill, Jen Robin, Carly Waters, Julianna Strickland, Cathleen Simmons, Lili Pettit, Ryan Eiesland and Brandie Larsen, and the countless others who believe that we are stronger together. Thank you to Wendy Schwartz and Kristi Bender of Cuff Home. Thank you to my awesome, ever-growing team: Deya Reece, Brand Manager Jennifer Callahan, Violet Dominguez, Katheryn Keller, Amanda Beaubien, Gomez Sandoval, and Ida Tasanen.

Eve Rodsky, it was a crazy trip to Vegas over eight years ago when you gave me the kick in the pants I needed to go for what I knew in my heart was my path. I hope every single person who reads this will check out her book *Fair Play*.

Thank you to my friends and family: Carolyn, Walter, Dave, Kat, Camile, Sarah, and Anya Fierson, Burton, Natalia and Gloria Leed, Serena Dimopoulos, Mary Beth Caccitolo, Lisa Boice, Shawna Boggie, Marilyn Shoemaker, Shana Waterman, Hopi James, and the countless others who have supported me through this journey.

Finally, a special thank you to all my clients, friends, and followers who have trusted me and my team in your homes. I am inspired by you every day, and my greatest joy is being in service to the unfolding of your lives. I am so full of gratitude.

RESOURCE GUIDE

APPS & SOFTWARE

1Password
1password.com
A secure password storage app that syncs across all your devices.

Asana
asana.com
A focused project and task management app.

Evernote
evernote.com
An app to keep notes and ideas organized at all times and across all your devices.

G Suite
gsuite.google.com
Email, Docs, Drive, and Calendar suite to optimize productivity for business.

Headspace
headspace.com
A meditation and mindfulness app for health and happiness on the go.

HomeZada
homezada.com
A digital home-management and inventory app.

Mailstrom
mailstrom.com
An app to clean out thousands of emails from your inbox as well as a tool to instantly unsubscribe to emails.

PaperKarma
paperkarma.com
An app to stop paper junk mail and catalogs.

Unroll.me
unroll.me
An app that offers a one-click unsubscribe and an option to roll up e-mail subscriptions into one email.

DONATION CENTERS

National Council of Jewish Women
ncjw.org/act/action/donate
A social justice organization for women, children, and families.

Habitat for Humanity
habitat.org/restores
An independently owned organization to help build strength, stability, self-reliance, and shelter in local communities.

Vietnam Veterans of America
vva.org/donate
An organization that offers home pickups, especially clothing for Vietnam Vets.

Out of the Closet Thrift Stores
outofthecloset.org
An organization that donates 96 cents of every dollar to HIV/AIDS services provided by AIDS Healthcare Foundation.

SERVICE PROVIDERS

TaskRabbit
taskrabbit.com
A service that offers help with anything you need done around the house.

Handy
handy.com
A service to instantly schedule cleaning and handyman tasks.

BOOKS

Newport, Cal. *Digital Minimalism: Choosing a Focused Life in Noisy World.* Portfolio/Penguin Random House, 2019.

McKeon, Greg. *Essentialism: The Disciplined Pursuit of Less.* Crown Business, 2014.

Millburn, Joshua Fields, and Ryan Nicodemus. *Everything That Remains: A Memoir by the Minimalists.* Asymmetrical Press, 2014.

Rees, Anuschka. *The Curated Closet: Discover Your Personal Style and Build Your Dream Wardrobe.* Ten Speed Press, 2017.

Kondō, Marie. *The Life Changing Magic of Tidying Up: The Japanese Art of Decluttering and Organizing.* Ten Speed Press, 2014.

Levitin, Daniel J. *The Organized Mind: Thinking Straight in the Age of Information Overload.* Dutton, 2016.

Carlson, Julie, and Margot Guralnick. *Remodelista: The Organized Home: Simple, Stylish Storage Ideas for All Over the House.* Artisan, 2017.

Payne, Kim John and Lisa M. Ross. *Simplicity Parenting: Using the Extraordinary Power of Less to Raise Calmer, Happier, and More Secure Kids.* Ballantine Books, 2010.

Henderson, Emily, and Angelina Borsics. *Styled: Secrets for Arranging Rooms, from Tabletops to Bookshelves.* Potter Style, 2015.

HOME FURNITURE & ACCESSORIES

CB2
cb2.com
Modern furniture, storage, and design services at an affordable price point.

Etsy
etsy.com
A unique, handmade, and vintage home decor online store for crafts.

Ferm Living
fermliving.com
Modern furniture and home accessories that meld form and function perfectly.

Hygge & West
hyggeandwest.com
A one-stop place for permanent and removable wallpaper in magical patterns for walls and inside drawers and cabinets.

Rejuvenation
rejuvenation.com
Quality, well-designed hardware, lighting, and decor for the home.

Room & Board
roomandboard.com
Modern, practical home furnishing and design services at reasonable prices.

Serena & Lily
serenaandlily.com
Simple, clean, California-chic home furniture for the perfect home oasis vibe.

Crate & Barrel + Crate & Barrel Kids
crateandbarrel.com
Functional and modern home furnishings plus fantastic storage solutions for kids.

Lulu & Georgia
luluandgeorgia.com
Furniture and home accessories in a variety of on-trend and up-to-date styles and materials.

Urban Outfitters
urbanoutfitters.com
Eclectic furniture and home accessories, plus out-of-the box storage solutions for every space.

West Elm
westelm.com
Modern home decor, wallpaper, and furniture. My favorite gallery of frames.

World Market
worldmarket.com
Eclectic furniture including a variety of baskets and storage solutions.

ORGANIZATIONAL SUPPLIES

The Container Store
containerstore.com
My go-to, one-stop shop for organizational tools and modular closets with a consistent inventory.

Golden Coil
goldencoil.com
Custom, spiral-bound planners and notebooks.

Ikea
ikea.com
Budget-friendly, modern, storage solutions and furniture.

Muji
muji.com
Simple, streamlined tools and accessories for everything you didn't know you needed to organize.

Staples
staples.com
Supplies and organizational tools for the office

Target
target.com
Rotating inventory of home furnishings, decor, and storage.

PHOTOS & MEMENTOS

Archival Methods
archivalmethods.com
Archival storage solutions for safekeeping mementos and precious photos.

Artkive
artkiveapp.com
Preserve kids' art in beautiful books by mail.

Artifact Uprising
artifactuprising.com
Beautifully designed and easy-to-make photobooks, frames, and photo keepsakes.

Framebridge
framebridge.com
Frames, gallery walls, and framed mementos without leaving the house.

Native Archival
nativearchival.com
Photo boxes and archival storage for photos, mementos, and memorabilia.

Mixbook
mixbook.com
User-friendly photobooks with extensive customization and style.

Savor
savor.us
Beautifully designed family keepsake storage boxes.

PROFESSIONAL ASSOCIATIONS

NAPO
napo.net
National Association of Productivity and Organizing Professionals.

APPO
appo.org
Professional organization: The Photo Organizers

Also visit
simplyspaced.com
for additional resources.

PRE-WORKSHEET

INTRODUCTION: START WITH THE END IN MIND

Pre-Worksheet	Checklist
Your three preferred charities are: ① _____ ② _____ ③ _____	☐ Brainstorm and research three local charities that accept donated items ☐ Identify your personal style by taking the Simply Spaced Style Quiz (www.simplyspaced.com/stylequiz)

What is your personal style?
☐ Minimalist
☐ Scandinavian
☐ Bohemian
☐ Industrial
☐ Zen
☐ Mid-Century Modern
☐ Modern
☐ Contemporary
☐ Rustic
☐ Retro
☐ Hollywood Glam
☐ Southwestern
☐ Coastal
☐ Eclectic
☐ Other
	☐ Create a Pinterest board to collect images of spaces, clothing, and designs that you love
	
	  ☐ *Bonus:* Check out the Simply Spaced Pinterest for inspiration
	
	  ☐ *Bonus:* Create a board for **each room** that you want to get organized (follow the chapters in this book or create your own)
	
	☐ Identify your Clutter Capacity for each member of your house by taking the quiz on page 18.
	
	☐ Grab a notebook. You'll want to capture all your inspired ideas in one dedicated place.

What is your clutter capacity? ☐ Gold ☐ Silver ☐ Bronze	
How do you feel about the current state of your home?	
What area of your home is causing you the most stress right now?	
How do you want your home to look, sound, smell, and feel?	
What would you do if you could unburden yourself from physical and mental clutter?	

CHAPTER 1 WORKSHEET: KITCHEN

STEP 1 – SIMPLIFY: DECLUTTER YOUR CHAOTIC KITCHEN

Worksheet 1	Checklist
How do you feel about the current state of your kitchen?	☐ Complete Worksheet 1 ☐ Set up your workspace ☐ Gather supplies: ☐ Notebook ☐ Pen ☐ Sharpie ☐ Post-its ☐ Trash bags ☐ Four bins or paper bags
How do you want your kitchen to look, feel, and smell?	☐ Label your bins: ☐ Donate ☐ Trash ☐ Recycle ☐ Other Room ☐ Other _____
What activities do you want to take place in your kitchen?	☐ Pull everything out and group like-with-like ☐ Process your items ☐ Wrap up ☐ Remove trash and recycle ☐ Put away "Other Room" items ☐ Deep clean/wipe down surfaces ☐ Find temporary homes for the items staying in this space ☐ Drop off donations
What are your diet and eating goals for this stage in your life? What are the diet and eating goals of your family?	**Note:** Use your notebook to track anything you need to do, replace, repair, or buy.
What are you willing to let go of in your kitchen?	

KITCHEN

STEP 2 – STREAMLINE: OPTIMIZE SPACE IN YOUR KITCHEN

Worksheet 2	Checklist

What organizational systems are working in your kitchen?	☐ Complete Worksheet 2
	
	☐ Create zones
	    ☐ Duplicate your Post-it notes (for each category you've identified)
	    ☐ Assign each category a zone by placing the Post-it note in its new home
	
	☐ Maximize space
	    ☐ Adjust shelving as needed
	    ☐ Inventory categories where product is needed
	    ☐ Take measurements as needed
	    ☐ Create a product list
	    ☐ Purchase new products for optimizing space

What's not working?	

What zones would be helpful in this space?	☐ Implement storage solutions
	    ☐ Install new product and put everything away in the new homes
	    ☐ Call a handyperson (if needed)
	
	☐ Label
	
	Note:
	Use your notebook to list your zones, inventory categories, take measurements, and to create your product list.

What areas could you rethink to optimize space (i.e. an empty vertical wall, unused deep storage, behind the door)?	

KITCHEN

STEP 3 – STYLE: CURATE A KITCHEN THAT'S THE HEART OF YOUR HOME

Worksheet 3	Checklist
What are three special items you can add or feature in your kitchen that will inspire you?	☐ Complete Worksheet 3 ☐ Feature beautiful pieces or heirlooms that can double as a utilitarian home ☐ Identify three favorite items to display ☐ Cull your everyday items and consider replacing them with more beautiful versions ☐ Add hooks and hanging shelves
What goals do you have for this space (i.e. painting, tiling, touch-ups, new curtains, pretty jars)?	Additional style tips to consider: ☐ Curate counters ☐ Decant ☐ Style with storage solutions
What new habits are you willing to implement?	
How can you involve your family/roommates in kitchen maintenance and the upkeep of the systems you've created?	

CHAPTER 2 WORKSHEET: BEDROOM

STEP 1 – SIMPLIFY: DECLUTTER YOUR BUSY BEDROOM

Worksheet 1	Checklist

How do you feel about the current state of your bedroom?	☐ Complete Worksheet 1
	
	  ☐ Set up your workspace
	    ☐ Gather supplies:
	      ☐ Notebook
	      ☐ Pen
	      ☐ Sharpie
	      ☐ Post-its
	      ☐ Trash bags
	      ☐ Four bins or paper bags

What do you want your bedroom to look, feel, and smell like?	☐ Label your bins:
	      ☐ Donate
	      ☐ Trash
	      ☐ Recycle
	      ☐ Other Room
	      ☐ Other_____
	
	☐ Pull everything out and group like-with-like

What activities do you want to take place in your bedroom? What activities does your partner want to take place in your bedroom?	☐ Process your items (remove anything that does not represent your current relationship or relationship goals)
	
	☐ Wrap up
	  ☐ Remove trash and recycle
	  ☐ Put away "Other Room" items
	  ☐ Deep clean/wipe down surfaces
	  ☐ Find temporary homes for the items staying in this space
	  ☐ Drop off donations

What are you unwilling to compromise on?	**Note:** Use your notebook to track anything you need to do, replace, repair, or buy.
What are you willing to let go of in your bedroom?	

BEDROOM

STEP 2 – STREAMLINE: OPTIMIZE SPACE IN YOUR BEDROOM

Worksheet 2	Checklist

What organizational systems are working in your bedroom?	☐ Complete Worksheet 2
	
	 ☐ Create zones
	     ☐ Duplicate your Post-it notes (for each category you've identified)
	     ☐ Assign each category a zone by placing the Post-it note in its new home
	
	 ☐ Maximize space
	     ☐ Adjust shelving as needed
	     ☐ Inventory categories where product is needed
	     ☐ Take measurements as needed
	     ☐ Create a product list
	     ☐ Purchase new products for optimizing space

What's not working?	☐ Implement storage solutions
	     ☐ Install new products and put everything away in their new homes
	     ☐ Call a handyperson (if needed)
	
	 ☐ Label
	
	 Note:
	 Use your notebook to list your zones, inventory categories, take measurements, and to create your product list.

What zones would be helpful in this space?	
What areas could you rethink to optimize space (i.e. an empty vertical wall, unused deep storage, behind the door)?	

BEDROOM

STEP 3 – STYLE: CURATE YOUR BEDROOM TO REFLECT YOU, YOUR PARTNER, AND YOUR GOALS

Worksheet 3	Checklist
What is your personal bedroom style?	☐ Complete Worksheet 3 ☐ Feature beautiful pieces or heirlooms that can double as a utilitarian home ☐ Identify three favorite items to display ☐ Cull your everyday items and consider replacing them with more beautiful versions ☐ Add hooks and hanging shelves
What is your partner's bedroom style?	Additional style tips to consider: ☐ Showcase your favorites ☐ Display with a tray ☐ Curate a gallery wall ☐ Rekindle the romance ☐ Layer your bed like a pro
What are three special items you can add or feature that will inspire your well-being or relationship daily?	
What new intentions do you have for this space?	

CHAPTER 3 WORKSHEET: CLOSET

STEP 1 – SIMPLIFY: DECLUTTER YOUR CRAMMED CLOSET

Worksheet 1	Checklist

How do you feel about the current state of your closet?	☐ Complete Worksheet 1
	
	☐ Set up your workspace
	   ☐ Gather supplies:
	      ☐ Notebook
	      ☐ Pen
	      ☐ Sharpie
	      ☐ Post-its
	      ☐ Trash bags
	      ☐ Four bins or paper bags

What do you want your closet to look, feel, and smell like?	☐ Label your bins:
	      ☐ Donate
	      ☐ Trash
	      ☐ Recycle
	      ☐ Other Room
	      ☐ Give to Mom

How do you want to feel when you get dressed?	☐ Sell
	      ☐ Repair
	      ☐ Fix
	      ☐ Dry clean
	      ☐ Other_____

What are the main activities or occasions that you dress for?	☐ Pull everything out and group like-with-like
	
	☐ Process your items
	
	☐ Wrap up
	   ☐ Remove trash and recycle
	   ☐ Put away "Other Room" items
	   ☐ Deep clean/wipe down surfaces
	   ☐ Find temporary homes for the items staying in this space
	   ☐ Drop off donations

What are your favorite, go-to brands?	**Note:** Use your notebook to track anything you need to do, replace, repair, or buy.
What are you willing to let go of in your closet?	

CLOSET

STEP 2 – STREAMLINE: OPTIMIZE SPACE IN YOUR CLOSET

Worksheet 2	Checklist

What organizational systems are working in your closet or wardrobe?	☐ Complete Worksheet 2
	
	☐ Create zones
	    ☐ Duplicate your Post-it notes (for each category you've identified)
	    ☐ Assign each category a zone by placing the Post-it note in its new home

What's not working?	☐ Maximize space
	    ☐ Adjust shelving as needed
	    ☐ Inventory categories where product is needed
	    ☐ Take measurements as needed
	    ☐ Create a product list
	    ☐ Purchase new products for optimizing space
	
	☐ Implement storage solutions
	    ☐ Install new product and put everything away in its new home
	    ☐ Call a handyperson (if needed)

What zones would be helpful in this space?	☐ Label **Note:** Use your notebook to list your zones, inventory categories, take measurements, and to create your product list.
What areas could you rethink to optimize space (i.e. an empty vertical wall, unused deep storage, behind the door)?	

CLOSET

STEP 3 – STYLE: CURATE YOUR CLOSET

Worksheet 3	Checklist
What is your personal clothing style(s)? ☐ Bohemian ☐ Modern minimalist ☐ Trendy ☐ Athleisure ☐ Classic/traditional ☐ Eclectic ☐ Feminine ☐ Grungy	☐ Complete Worksheet 3 ☐ Feature beautiful pieces or heirlooms that can double as a utilitarian home ☐ Identify three favorite items to display ☐ Cull your everyday items and consider replacing them with more beautiful versions ☐ Add hooks and hanging shelves Additional style tips to consider:
What common occasions do you need to get dressed for?	☐ Swap out your mismatched hangers ☐ Pair ten outfits that you love ☐ Invest in your quality basics ☐ Create a display ☐ File-fold
What are three special items you can add or feature that will inspire you to maintain this space?	
What new goals do you have for this space? Do you want a capsule wardrobe, boutique-style vibe, or more sustainable purchases?	

CHAPTER 4 WORKSHEET: BATH AND BEAUTY

STEP 1 – SIMPLIFY: DECLUTTER YOUR BRIMMING BATHROOM

Worksheet 1	Checklist
How do you feel about the current state of your bathroom?	☐ Complete Worksheet 1 ☐ Set up your workspace 　☐ Gather supplies: 　　☐ Notebook 　　☐ Pen 　　☐ Sharpie 　　☐ Post-its 　　☐ Trash bags 　　☐ Four bins or paper bags
What do you want your bathroom to look, feel, and smell like?	☐ Label your bins: 　　☐ Donate 　　☐ Trash 　　☐ Recycle 　　☐ Other Room 　　☐ Other_____ ☐ Pull everything out and group like-with-like
What activities do you want to take place in your bathroom (besides the obvious)?	☐ Process your items ☐ Wrap up 　☐ Remove trash and recycle 　☐ Safely recycle expired medications 　☐ Put away "Other Room" items 　☐ Deep clean/wipe down surfaces 　☐ Find temporary homes for the items staying in this space 　☐ Drop off donations
What are your favorite, go-to brands or products?	**Note:** Use your notebook to track anything you need to do, replace, repair, or buy.
What are you willing to let go of in your bathroom?	

BATH AND BEAUTY

STEP 2 – STREAMLINE: OPTIMIZE SPACE IN YOUR BATHROOM

Worksheet 2	Checklist

What organizational systems are working in your bathroom?	☐ Complete Worksheet 2
	
	 ☐ Create zones
	     ☐ Duplicate your Post-it notes (for each category you've identified)
	     ☐ Assign each category a zone by placing the Post-it note in its new home
	
	 ☐ Maximize space
	     ☐ Adjust shelving as needed
	     ☐ Inventory categories where product is needed
	     ☐ Take measurements as needed
	     ☐ Create a product list
	     ☐ Purchase new products for optimizing space

What's not working?	☐ Implement storage solutions
	     ☐ Install new product and put everything away in its new home
	     ☐ Call a handyperson (if needed)
	
	 ☐ Label
	
	 Note:
	 Use your notebook to list your zones, inventory categories, take measurements, and to create your product list.

What zones would be helpful in this space?	
What areas could you rethink to optimize space (i.e. an empty vertical wall, unused deep storage, behind the door)?	

BATH AND BEAUTY

STEP 3 – STYLE: CURATE YOUR CALMING BATHROOM

Worksheet 3	Checklist
What special items can you add to make your bathroom feel like a spa?	☐ Complete Worksheet 3 ☐ Feature beautiful pieces or heirlooms that can double as a utilitarian home ☐ Identify three favorite items to display ☐ Cull your everyday items and consider replacing them with more beautiful versions ☐ Add hooks and hanging shelves
What new intentions do you have for this space?	Additional style tips to consider: ☐ Replace worn towels and rags with plush light-colored or white towels ☐ Add some plant life ☐ Add candles, salts, and specialty scrubs ☐ Streamline products
What are three special items you can add or feature that will inspire you to maintain this space?	☐ Swap out shower curtain and bath mat ☐ Style with natural materials
What new goals do you have for this space? (i.e., take more baths, take time to get ready in the morning, paint)?	

CHAPTER 5 WORKSHEET: LIVING SPACES

STEP 1 – SIMPLIFY: DECLUTTER YOUR UNLIVABLE LIVING SPACES

Worksheet 1	Checklist

How do you feel about the current state of your living areas?	☐ Complete Worksheet 1
	
	☐ Set up your workspace
	  ☐ Gather supplies:
	    ☐ Notebook
	    ☐ Pen
	    ☐ Sharpie
	    ☐ Post-its
	    ☐ Trash bags
	    ☐ Four bins or paper bags

What do you want your living areas to look, feel, and smell like?	☐ Label your bins:
	    ☐ Donate
	    ☐ Trash
	    ☐ Recycle
	    ☐ Other Room
	    ☐ Other _____
	
	☐ Pull everything out and group like-with-like

What activities do you want to take place in your living areas?	☐ Process your items
	
	☐ Wrap up
	  ☐ Remove trash and recycle
	  ☐ Put away "Other Room" items
	  ☐ Deep clean/wipe down surfaces
	  ☐ Find temporary homes for the items staying in this space
	  ☐ Drop off donations

What are your social or entertaining goals at home for this stage in your life?	**Note:** Use your notebook to track anything you need to do, replace, repair, or buy.
What are you willing to let go of in your living space?	

LIVING SPACES

STEP 2 – STREAMLINE: OPTIMIZE SPACE IN YOUR LIVING AREAS

Worksheet 2	Checklist

What organizational systems are working in your living space?
 	
What's not working?
 	
What zones would be helpful in this space?
 	
What areas could you rethink to optimize space (i.e. an empty vertical wall, unused deep storage, behind the door)?
	☐ Complete Worksheet 2
	
	☐ Create zones
	   ☐ Duplicate your Post-it notes (for each category you've identified)
	   ☐ Assign each category a zone by placing the Post-it note in its new home
	
	☐ Maximize space
	   ☐ Adjust shelving as needed
	   ☐ Inventory categories where product is needed
	   ☐ Take measurements as needed
	   ☐ Create a product list
	   ☐ Purchase new products for optimizing space
	
	☐ Implement storage solutions
	   ☐ Install new product and put everything away in its new home
	   ☐ Call a handyperson (if needed)
	
	☐ Label
	
	Note:
	Use your notebook to list your zones, inventory categories, take measurements, and to create your product list.

LIVING SPACES

STEP 3 – STYLE: CURATE YOUR LIVING SPACES

Worksheet 3	Checklist
What are three special items you can add or feature that will inspire your living space?	☐ Complete Worksheet 3 ☐ Feature beautiful pieces or heirlooms that can double as a utilitarian home ☐ Identify three favorite items to display ☐ Cull your everyday items and consider replacing them with more beautiful versions ☐ Add hooks and hanging shelves
What new goals do you have for your living space?	Additional style tips to consider: ☐ Frame a favorite photo ☐ Make your pillows talk ☐ Add plants ☐ Update lighting ☐ Choose your color palette
How can you involve your family/roommate in communal space maintenance?	
What colors inspire you and feel warm in this space?	

CHAPTER 6 WORKSHEET: KIDS' SPACES

STEP 1 – SIMPLIFY: DECLUTTER YOUR KIDS' CHAOTIC ROOM OR PLAYROOM

Worksheet 1	Checklist

How do you feel about the current state of your kids' space(s)?	☐ Complete Worksheet 1
	
	☐ Set up your workspace
	    ☐ Gather supplies:
	        ☐ Notebook
	        ☐ Pen
	        ☐ Sharpie
	        ☐ Post-its
	        ☐ Trash bags
	        ☐ Four bins or paper bags

How do you want your kids to participate in this process?	☐ Label your bins:
	        ☐ Donate
	        ☐ Trash
	        ☐ Recycle
	        ☐ Other Room
	        ☐ Other _____
	
	☐ Pull everything out and group like-with-like

What activities do you want to take place in your kids' space(s)?	☐ Process your items
	    ☐ Remove all objects that do not support your child's imagination, learning, or growth
	
	☐ Wrap up
	    ☐ Remove trash and recycle
	    ☐ Put away "Other Room" items
	    ☐ Deep clean/wipe down surfaces

What are your goals for your kids at this stage in their lives?	☐ Find temporary homes for the items staying in this space ☐ Drop off donations **Note:** Use your notebook to track anything you need to do, replace, repair, or buy.
What are you willing to let go of in your kids' space(s)?	

KIDS' SPACES

STEP 2 – STREAMLINE: OPTIMIZE SPACE IN YOUR KIDS' ROOM OR PLAYROOM

Worksheet 2	Checklist
What organizational systems are working in your kids' space?	☐ Complete Worksheet 2 ☐ Create zones 　☐ Duplicate your Post-it notes (for each category you've identified) 　☐ Assign each category a zone by placing the Post-it note in its new home ☐ Maximize space 　☐ Adjust shelving as needed 　☐ Inventory categories where product is needed 　☐ Take measurements as needed 　☐ Create a product list 　☐ Purchase new products for optimizing space
What's not working?	☐ Implement storage solutions 　☐ Install new product and put everything away in the new homes 　☐ Call a handyperson (if needed) ☐ Label
What zones would be helpful in this space?	**Note:** Use your notebook to list your zones, inventory categories, take measurements, and to create your product list.
What areas could you rethink to optimize space (i.e. an empty vertical wall, unused deep storage, behind the door)?	

KIDS' SPACES

STEP 3 – STYLE: CURATE YOUR KIDS' ROOM OR PLAYROOM

Worksheet 3	Checklist
What is unique about your child or his or her personal style?	☐ Complete Worksheet 3 ☐ Feature beautiful pieces or heirlooms that can double as a utilitarian home ☐ Identify three favorite items to display ☐ Cull your everyday items and consider replacing them with more beautiful versions ☐ Add hooks and hanging shelves
What are three special items you can add or feature that will inspire your child's well-being or family relationships every day?	Additional style tips to consider: ☐ Create a kid-friendly gallery wall ☐ Put puzzles on display ☐ Unbox games ☐ Display wooden toys ☐ Embrace the rainbow
What intentions do you have for this space?	
How can you involve your family in the maintenance and upkeep of the systems you've created?	

CHAPTER 7 WORKSHEET: STORAGE AND UTLILTY SPACES

STEP 1 – SIMPLIFY: DECLUTTER YOUR UNSIGHTLY STORAGE SPACE

Worksheet 1	Checklist

How do you feel about the current state of your storage area?	☐ Complete Worksheet 1
	
	☐ Set up your workspace
	  ☐ Gather supplies:
	    ☐ Notebook
	    ☐ Pen
	    ☐ Sharpie
	    ☐ Post-its
	    ☐ Trash bags
	    ☐ Four bins or paper bags

What do you want your storage area to look, feel, and smell like?	☐ Label your bins:
	    ☐ Donate
	    ☐ Trash
	    ☐ Recycle
	    ☐ Other Room
	    ☐ Other _____
	
	☐ Pull everything out and group like-with-like

What activities do you want to take place in your storage area?	☐ Process your items
	
	☐ Wrap up
	  ☐ Remove trash and recycle
	  ☐ Put away "Other Room" items
	  ☐ Deep clean/wipe down surfaces
	  ☐ Find temporary homes for the items staying in this space
	  ☐ Drop off donations

What is the function of this storage area?	**Note:** Use your notebook to track anything you need to do, replace, repair, or buy.
What are you willing to let go of in your storage area?	

STORAGE AND UTLILTY SPACES

STEP 2 – STREAMLINE: OPTIMIZE SPACE IN YOUR STORAGE AREAS

Worksheet 2	Checklist

What organizational systems are working in your storage area?	☐ Complete Worksheet 2
	
	☐ Create zones
	   ☐ Duplicate your Post-it notes (for each category you've identified)
	   ☐ Assign each category a zone by placing the Post-it note in its new home
	
	☐ Maximize space
	   ☐ Adjust shelving as needed
	   ☐ Inventory categories where product is needed
	   ☐ Take measurements as needed
	   ☐ Create a product list
	   ☐ Purchase new products for optimizing space

What's not working?	

What zones would be helpful in this space?	☐ Implement storage solutions
	   ☐ Install new product and put everything away in the new homes
	   ☐ Call a handyperson (if needed)
	
	☐ Label
	
	Note:
	Use your notebook to list your zones, inventory categories, take measurements, and to create your product list.

What areas could you rethink to optimize space (i.e. an empty vertical wall, unused deep storage, behind the door)?	

STORAGE AND UTLILTY SPACES

STEP 3 – STYLE: CURATE YOUR SUSTAINABLE STORAGE SPACE

Worksheet 3	Checklist
What are three special items you can add or feature in your storage areas that will that will inspire you?	☐ Complete Worksheet 3 ☐ Feature beautiful pieces or heirlooms that can double as a utilitarian home ☐ Identify three favorite items to display ☐ Cull your everyday items and consider replacing them with more beautiful versions ☐ Add hooks and hanging shelves
What goals do you have for this space (i.e. painting, tiling, touch-ups, new curtains, pretty jars)?	Additional style tips to consider: ☐ Upgrade your whole system ☐ Add a pegboard wall ☐ Add wallpaper ☐ Tidy your tools ☐ Go big on your walls
What new habits are you willing to implement?	
How can you involve your family or roommates in the maintenance and upkeep of the systems you've created?	

CHAPTER 8 WORKSHEET: OFFICE

STEP 1 – SIMPLIFY: DECLUTTER YOUR OUT-OF-CONTROL OFFICE

Worksheet 1	Checklist

How do you feel about the current state of your office?	☐ Complete Worksheet 1
	
	☐ Set up your workspace
	   ☐ Gather supplies:
	      ☐ Notebook
	      ☐ Pen
	      ☐ Sharpie
	      ☐ Post-its
	      ☐ Trash bags
	      ☐ Four bins or paper bags

What do you want your office to look, feel, and smell like?	☐ Label your bins:
	      ☐ Donate
	      ☐ Trash
	      ☐ Recycle
	      ☐ Other Room
	      ☐ Other _____
	
	☐ Pull everything out and group like-with-like

What activities do you want to take place in your office?	☐ Process your items
	
	☐ Wrap up
	   ☐ Remove trash and recycle
	   ☐ Put away "Other Room" items
	   ☐ Deep clean/wipe down surfaces
	   ☐ Find temporary homes for the items staying in this space
	   ☐ Drop off donations

What are your work or career goals for this stage in your life?	**Note:** Use your notebook to track anything you need to do, replace, repair, or buy.
What are you willing to let go of in your office?	

OFFICE

STEP 2 – STREAMLINE: OPTIMIZE SPACE IN YOUR OFFICE

Worksheet 2	Checklist

What organizational systems are working in your office?	☐ Complete Worksheet 2
	
	 ☐ Create zones
	    ☐ Duplicate your Post-it notes (for each category you've identified)
	    ☐ Assign each category a zone by placing the Post-it note in its new home
	
	 ☐ Maximize space
	    ☐ Adjust shelving as needed
	    ☐ Inventory categories where product is needed
	    ☐ Take measurements as needed
	    ☐ Create a product list
	    ☐ Purchase new products for optimizing space

What's not working?	☐ Implement storage solutions
	    ☐ Install new product and put everything away in the new homes
	    ☐ Call a handyperson (if needed)
	
	 ☐ Label

What zones would be helpful in this space?	**Note:** Use your notebook to list your zones, inventory categories, take measurements, and to create your product list.
What areas could you rethink to optimize space (i.e. an empty vertical wall, unused deep storage, behind the door)?	

OFFICE

STEP 3 – STYLE: CURATE YOUR INSPIRING OFFICE

Worksheet 3	Checklist
What are three special items you can add or feature in your office that will inspire you?	☐ Complete Worksheet 3 ☐ Feature beautiful pieces or heirlooms that can double as a utilitarian home ☐ Identify three favorite items to display ☐ Cull your everyday items and consider replacing them with more beautiful versions ☐ Add hooks and hanging shelves
What goals do you have for this space (i.e. painting, touch-ups, new desk)?	Additional style tips to consider: ☐ Upgrade your storage ☐ Mix materials ☐ Display your daily inspo ☐ Rethink your walls ☐ Get the right desk & chair
What new habits are you willing to implement?	
How can you involve your family or roommates in home office maintenance and upkeep of the systems you've created?	

CHAPTER 9 WORKSHEET: PAPER

STEP 1 – SIMPLIFY: DECLUTTER YOUR PAPER PILE-UP

Worksheet 1	Checklist

How do you feel about the current state of your papers?	☐ Complete Worksheet 1
	
	☐ Set up your workspace
	    ☐ Gather supplies:
	        ☐ Notebook
	        ☐ Post-its
	        ☐ File bin or file box
	        ☐ Hanging files
	        ☐ Three-inch transparent tabs
	        ☐ Three-inch colored tabs
	        ☐ File inserts
	        ☐ Label maker
	        ☐ Sorting bins
	        ☐ Sorting bin labels
	        ☐ Binder clips
	        ☐ Letter opener

What do you want to feel when you encounter a paper pile in your home?	☐ Label your bins:
	        ☐ Recycle
	        ☐ Shred
	        ☐ Digitize
	        ☐ To-do
	        ☐ Other _____

What is your current process for handling paper as it enters your home?	☐ Pull everything out and group like-with-like
	
	☐ Process your paper
	    ☐ Make active files
	    ☐ Make accessible files
	    ☐ Archive

What is your ultimate objective for paper processing? For example, do you want to go paperless or get everything filled and archived?	☐ Wrap up
	    ☐ Remove trash and recycle
	    ☐ Shred papers or take them to a shredding facility
	    ☐ Scan or digitize any papers that can go paperless

What are you willing to let go of to make that a reality?	**Note:** Use your notebook to track anything you need to do, replace, repair, or buy.

PAPER

STEP 2 – STREAMLINE: OPTIMIZE YOUR PAPER-PROCESSING SYSTEMS

Worksheet 2	Checklist

What organizational papers systems are working in your home?	☐ Complete Worksheet 2
	
	☐ Create zones
	  ☐ Identify the areas in your home where you want paper to land
	  ☐ Assign each zone its intended task (i.e. mail sorting, bill paying, filing, storing)

What's not working?	☐ Maximize space
	  ☐ Inventory categories where product is needed
	  ☐ Take measurements as needed
	  ☐ Create a product list
	  ☐ Purchase new products for optimizing space
	
	☐ Implement storage solutions
	  ☐ Install new product and file your paperwork

Where do you naturally process paperwork?	☐ Label **Note:** Use your notebook to list your zones, inventory categories, take measurements, and to create your product list.
What can you change or add to make processing paperwork easier or more appealing (i.e. a desk and chair, a mail station, an active filing system)?	

PAPER

STEP 3 – STYLE: CURATE YOUR PAPER-PROCESSING STATION

Worksheet 3	Checklist
Would you be more inspired to maintain your paper systems if you had a stylish system and tools to work with?	☐ Complete Worksheet 3 ☐ Replace mismatched containers, sorters, and paper storage with a cohesive set ☐ Upgrade your paper storage with label plates or handwritten labels ☐ Use 3-inch tabs ☐ Curate an inspiration board
What paper categories can you keep out and style into your space?	☐ Replace mismatched file folders, labels, and files with white ones for calm cohesion
What paper categories do you want to add to your active files?	
What paper categories do you want to archive?	

CHAPTER 10 WORKSHEET: PHOTOS

STEP 1 – SIMPLIFY: DECLUTTER YOUR PILE OF PRECIOUS PICTURES

Worksheet 1	Checklist

How do you feel about the current state of your printed photo collection?	☐ Complete Worksheet 1
	☐ Set up your workspace
	   ☐ Gather supplies:
	      ☐ Notebook
	      ☐ Pen
	      ☐ Sharpie
	      ☐ Post-its
	      ☐ Rubber bands
	      ☐ Four to five sorting bins
	   ☐ Optional extras:
	      ☐ Dental floss
	      ☐ White cotton gloves
	      ☐ Photo pencil
	      ☐ Index cards
	      ☐ Photo box
	      ☐ Artkive box
	   ☐ Label your bins:
	      ☐ Trash
	      ☐ Recycle
	      ☐ Digitize
	      ☐ Other_____
	
	☐ Pull everything out and group like-with-like
	☐ Process your photos and categorize
	☐ Wrap up

What would you like to do with your printed photos once they are organized and digitized? ☐ Create digital albums to share with family ☐ Make a slideshow or video ☐ Create a gallery wall or frame prints ☐ Scrapbook ☐ Photo gifts ☐ Create photo books ☐ Traditional albums ☐ Other_____	
Where do you want to store your scanned photos? ☐ (i.e. Google Drive, iCloud, Dropbox, OneDrive etc.) ☐ External Hard Drive or thumb drive at home ☐ Safety Deposit box ☐ Other_____	**Note:** Use your notebook to track anything want to frame, hang, share, or restore.
What types of photo media do you have? ☐ Printed photos_____ ☐ Slides____ _____ ☐ Negatives_____ ☐ 8mm film_____ ☐ 16mm film_____ ☐ Super 8_____ ☐ DVDs_____ ☐ Thumb drives_____ ☐ DVDs_____ ☐ SD cards_____ ☐ Hard drives _____ ☐ Other_____	

PHOTOS

STEP 2 – STREAMLINE: OPTIMIZE YOUR PHOTO COLLECTION

Worksheet 2	Checklist
What about your current printed photo collection is not working?	☐ Complete Worksheet 2 ☐ Double check your collection ☐ Scan your photos ☐ Identify and cull your favorite photos ☐ Back up your collection ☐ Implement storage ☐ Label
How do you want to digitize your photo collection (i.e. scan yourself or hire a company)?	
Do you have any favorite photos or groups of photos that you want to flag for framing, display, or a photobook?	
Approximately how many photos do you have (a one inch stack is about 100 photos)?	

STEP 3 – STYLE: CURATE YOUR PHOTO COLLECTION

Worksheet 3	Checklist
Do you like to have photos of your friends and family up in your home?	☐ Complete Worksheet 3 ☐ Curate a gallery wall ☐ Create photo books with your newly organized photos ☐ Style your shelves with photos ☐ Create a shareable album, video, or slideshow
Are the photos that are displayed in your home an accurate reflection of your life right now?	
What rooms in your home could use a photo refresh?	

CHAPTER 11 WORKSHEET: MEMENTOS

STEP 1 – SIMPLIFY: DECLUTTER YOUR MEMENTO AND MEMORABILIA MESS

Worksheet 1	Checklist

How do you feel about the current state of your mementos?	☐ Complete Worksheet 1
	☐ Set up your workspace
	  ☐ Gather supplies:
	    ☐ Notebook
	    ☐ Pen
	    ☐ Sharpie
	    ☐ Post-its
	    ☐ Trash bags
	    ☐ Four bins or paper bags
	  ☐ Label your bins:
	    ☐ Trash
	    ☐ Recycle
	    ☐ Other Room
	    ☐ Other_____

What do you want to do with your mementos?	☐ Pull everything out and group like-with-like ☐ Process your mementos and categorize ☐ Wrap up ☐ Remove trash and recycle ☐ Put away "Other Room" items ☐ Deep clean/wipe down surfaces ☐ Find temporary homes for the items staying in this space
What are you willing to let go of in your collection?	**Note:** Use your notebook to track anything you want to photograph, frame, digitize, or display.
How many boxes of mementos do you want to have for each member of the family for each year? In ten years?	

MEMENTOS

STEP 2 – STREAMLINE: OPTIMIZE YOUR MEMENTO STORAGE

Worksheet 2	Checklist
What systems are already working to keep your mementos organized?	☐ Complete Worksheet 2 ☐ Create zones ☐ Maximize space ☐ Implement storage solutions ☐ Label
What's not working?	
How many memento boxes will you need for this year?	**Note:** Use your notebook to list your zones, inventory the types of mementos you have, and to create your product list.

STEP 3 – STYLE: CURATE YOUR MEMENTOS

Worksheet 3	Checklist
What are your favorite memories?	☐ Complete Worksheet 3 ☐ Display three things you love ☐ Create art and memory books ☐ Frame special objects ☐ Make a memory blanket
What kinds of mementos do you like to collect?	
What are some ideas you've had or learned about for displaying mementos?	
How would you like to pass on or share your saved mementos (i.e. storage boxes, memory books)?